Whaddayah Mean
Leave Home and Travel
for the Rest of My Life!

The Guide to Pre-Retirement RV Living

About the Authors

Gene and Deanne Townsend are full-time RV travellers who, at ages too young to retire were advised by other full-timers, "If you're gonna do it, go for it while you're young!"

Thus they sold it all and hit the road, knowing that it would mean having to work for at least 20 more years. They loved the concept of making the entire continent their home, and accepted the challenge wholeheartedly! Now, years later, they are eager to share with you the pros and cons of this lifestyle of freedom; telling you of the promises that are out there for you—as well as the mistakes they made.

Gene and Deanne make their living by presenting full-timing seminars throughout the U.S. Deanne also ministers in song and teaching concerts in Christian organizations, while Gene keeps her going with the "technical stuff," and selling tapes and books. Writing books, magazine articles, and technical literature rounds out their "gypsy" way of earning their keep.

Whaddayah Mean Leave Home and Travel for the Rest of My Life!

second edition

The Guide to Pre-Retirement RV Living

Gene and Deanne Townsend

Wilderness Adventure Books

ISBN: 0-923568-40-9
Former ISBN: 0-923568-21-2

Cover photograph by Kenneth Poertner

Published by:

 Wilderness Adventure Books
P.O. Box 217
Davisburg, Michigan 48350

Library of Congress Cataloging-in-Publication Data

Townsend, Harold E. and Deanne M.
Whaddayah Mean Leave Home and Travel For the Rest of My Life / Gene and Deanne Townsend.
Includes bibliographical references and index.
ISBN: 0-923568-40-9 : $13.95
1. Mobile home living—United States. I. Title.
TX1107.T69 1995
796.7'9—dc20

Manufactured in the United States of America

*To our children, grandchildren,
and all our generations to come.
May you live all your dreams to the fullest!*

And to Jesus Christ, who makes it all possible.

CONTENTS

SECTION II: GET SET!

Section IV. Enjoy Yourself!

FOREWORD

Greg and Debbie Robus, *Workamper News*

If you are considering full-time RV'ing, this book is a "must-read." The Townsends have covered the practical side of selling everything and "taking to the road," and they explain it all in an enjoyable, easy-to-read manner. If you haven't included this book in your preparations for full-timing, we have to ask, "Whaddayah Mean?!"

Debbie Robus, Publisher
Workamper News

PREFACE

"Happy is the man that findeth wisdom, and the man that getteth understanding."
Proverbs 3:13

It was a beautiful day in September 1987. The California sun was warm, and though the matching blue sky was tinged with smog, we were happy.

Our day had come! All the children were grown and married and had left home. We had just sold our house and everything in it and invested our money. We had a thirty-six foot Coachman motorhome with all of our best things in place. Our "rig" had been road-tested, camp-tested, and upgraded (as far as we knew) for full-time RV living.

Shouting "So long!" to all of our neighbors and the home where we had lived for over seventeen years, we were on the road toward our exciting new life.

Although we had not yet reached the conventional retirement age, our days of working nine-to-five were over. We had chosen to make America our home, and work at whatever, and wherever, we wanted. Perhaps we would have to face lean times as we learned the pros and cons of this new lifestyle. However, we were relatively young, mentally resilient, and confident we could survive whatever befell us.

That "befelling" was to begin much sooner than we anticipated. That day, as we drove through the dry upper deserts of California, we passed through an area where numerous grass and brush fires had been reported—which also happened to be burning alongside the road.

It was a bit scary, and became even more frightening when our smoke alarm started beeping. Deanne checked the system and blew into it, confident that the clamor was caused by the smoke from the fires. Unable to stop it, she assumed that the smoke from outside was too heavy to keep it cleared, and the beeping continued rhythmically until we arrived at our first campsite. We have since learned to remove the battery to silence the alarm, after making sure there is no fire and it is safe to do so.

As we pulled into the park, a man ran over to us shouting, "You're leaking something under the motorhome—it looks like gasoline!" Climbing down and looking under the motorhome, Gene found a steady stream of gasoline running onto the ground, only inches away from the hot exhaust pipe! He quickly shut off the engine and crawled underneath, where he discovered the gas line to the rear tank had separated. The rubber hose, which the factory had used for a gas line, had been pulled too tightly and the coupling had separated. We had just poured about twenty-five gallons of gasoline onto the freeway as we drove through those fires. What we had assumed was the beeping of our smoke alarm had been the alarm raised by our LP gas detector, which was activated by the fumes from the gasoline.

Not only that, but an examination of our entire rig revealed that we had almost lost our S-10 pickup, which was being towed behind the motorhome. It was missing a safety pin holding a hitch-pin in place. When the hitch-pin was installed, the new tow-bar attachment on the front of the truck had merely been bolted in place. The bolts had allowed the yoke to pivot around and apparently break or shear the pin. Close call—this has since been corrected with a quick trip to a local welding shop.

Was this a sample of how our new life would be? We were to learn that, yes, it would be a continual experience of fixing things (just as it had been at home). The difference would be in the *kinds* of repairs. No dishwasher would flood the kitchen floor, but due to the constant movement of our new home, different things would break, leak, or wear out.

But we also experienced joys that never would have been possible if we had been afraid to "leave home." Much happiness would make up for the occasional discouragements that are part of every lifestyle.

It was only a month later, on a Sunday afternoon, while driving through Oklahoma, that we remarked how contented we were. Each of us was experiencing our favorite things. Gene was driving the motorhome (his favorite pastime) and listening to a football game (his favorite sport) on the radio. Deanne had spread the Sunday paper (her favorite relaxation reading) across her side of the driving area, and had put popcorn (her favorite food) in the microwave to pop as we traveled. And it was raining (the favorite weather for both of us). What could be better? All this and freedom, too.

It is now several years later, and we have learned much about living in an RV full-time. Like any other kind of life, it has its challenges. But America is full of sights that we may never have gotten to see had we not struck out on our own. True, we've often gotten into situations that have caused us to wonder if we could survive. But never have we wished we hadn't come.

If you're wondering if this is the life for you, please join us as we share information about this gypsy lifestyle, in hopes that we can make your road smoother. This book will answer such questions as how to choose your home state, where to vote, how to pay your taxes and to whom, and what to see and do. It will also suggest some methods to finance your "dream-come-true" lifestyle.

There are thousands of us on the road. Although we live a life that is outside society's norm, it is perfectly viable. Come join us. As they say in the song—we've only just begun . . . to live!

Section I:

On Your Mark!

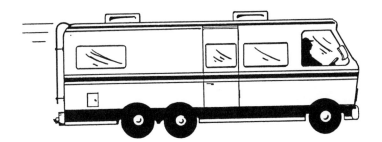

1

You Mean *Camp* Forever?

"Can two walk together, except they be agreed?" Amos 3:3

Convincing Your Mate

Deanne was perfectly happy living the life of the typical American mother and wife. A house, two cars, and a TV in every conceivable room—with dual jobs and monthly payments to match. Wasn't that all that expected in the 1980s? Keeping up with the Joneses (who were trying to keep up with the Smiths) was all part of the game.

Camping had always been a part of our lives, but then Gene read about people who actually *lived* in RVs and traveled full-time. He remembered a co-worker and his wife whom he had met as a Field Engineer. They lived in a camp trailer as the husband traveled from assignment to assignment. Was it possible for us to enjoy such a life while we were still young enough to work?

Unease is typical in almost every case where the suggestion of leaving your stationary home and into a moving one is considered—leaving security, kids, and grandkids behind; to share your life with strangers in places where you don't even know how to spell the name or where to find the grocery store. "It just isn't something that could be done." Deanne declared. "Not actually—not by us!" She admits it took two to three months for her even to

understand this new proposition. Then another six months to admit
to herself (let alone to Gene) that we were actually going to do it.

How did Gene convince her? By going RV shopping "just to
look." You know—Disneyland for adults. Little by little, Deanne
saw that today's RVs have everything her house did—and at about
the same price. Mentally, she began to place all of her belongings
within each one. In this manner, we eventually found and purchased
our very own "home."

After shopping around and reading magazine articles and trave-
logues, we visited with others who lived such a life (or wanted to)
whenever we were out "camping." That was enough to convince us
we couldn't wait to get on the road.

100% Versus Partial Full-Timing

Gene remembers that it took somewhat more work to get Deanne
from the idea of "part-time (or partial) full-timing" to "100% full-
timing." As we define it, "full-timers" are people who *live* in their
RV for any length of time during the year. If you live in your RV
year 'round, that is called 100%. If you only live some part of the
year in your RV, it is called partial, or part-time, full-timing. To
simplify this book, however, we'll call anyone who lives in, versus
just camps in, their RV, a "full-timer."

At first, Deanne was willing to travel for three or four months
at a time, but still felt she had to come home occasionally. So what
changed her mind? Thinking about the different kinds of work that
could be done on the road (which didn't require coming back to a
nine-to-five job every few months) really helped. Also, we realized
it would be more fun to come "back home" to visit our children and
grandchildren whenever we wanted to—for as long as we wanted
to—or not at all if we didn't want to.

We have found that as we grow older, time goes by much more
quickly, and living our dream becomes more important to us than
being the biggest and/or the best. So we encourage you: However
you want to do it—whatever you want to call it—reach out! Grab
the brass ring before it's too late. Do it—it's your life. Live it to its
fullest.

What Kind of People Make Successful Full-Timers?

We realize that it takes all kinds of horses (and people) to make a horse race—and just so, many people are not cut out for full-time travel. People we've met on the road have come from every conceivable background. They like to do as many different kinds of things, both in work and play, as there are people to do them. We have also discovered that the one trait they have in common is the ability to be happy within themselves—secure, no matter what their surroundings or circumstances.

All of us miss familiar people and places, but generally, full-timers are confident in the knowledge that life can be very confining if you live for things and/or other people, rather than doing whatever it is that you want to do.

Something else we had to consider when we decided to work and play in equal time frames was that we would be constantly working and playing together. We would no longer leave each other in the morning and go to work, and return to be together only in the evening hours and on weekends.

As retirees can tell you, this can put a strain on any marriage if you and your spouse/traveling friend are not compatible. We have to admit that sometimes we need time and space alone—especially since we do the same kind of work, and find ourselves treading on each other's turf when putting together a project. Thus, we *make* the time with private walks, splitting up tasks such as laundry, working on the car or sometimes just going into separate rooms, so we have time to think alone.

Just be aware: If you and your spouse/traveling friend don't get along too well, you might find this type of life too stressful on your relationship.

Most Common Complaint

As we have talked to full-timers, the most common complaint we've heard is, "If I had it to do over, I would have done it sooner. Before the arthritis that now makes it impossible to walk or run, and before my heart problem that keeps me from climbing the hills." So we decided: Instead of staying at home and working until the motorhome was paid for—which would put off traveling until perhaps we were too old or sick to go—we would continue to work and pay off the motorhome on the road while we enjoyed the travel. Instead of steadily working fifty weeks and playing steadily for the other two—we would mix work and play for fifty-two weeks a year.

Since we have each left our forties and the general good health of our youth, and entered into our fifties, we have again proven this reasoning. We have seen many of our friends meet with the typical illnesses of age—and some have even passed away. It was a good decision; we're glad we made it.

Presenting seminars is one way of earning a living on the road.

Commitment to your Dream—What Price Security?

It took real commitment to our dream to leave behind the known and comfortable security of our home, steady income, our children and grandchildren, and many friends. For us, that security came at such a high price, we were not willing to pay it. After all, we were talking about our lives versus our things. And our time for enjoying life was moving faster and faster. The time for us to make the decision was now.

What If It Doesn't Work?

In any crowd, when someone asks us what we do, as we begin to explain how we live, it seems that there are a hundred questions. Always, someone in that crowd says they are planning or hoping to do the same when "that day" comes. More often that not, "that day" is always in the future. Though they may know (or may only be subconsciously aware) that they may never do it, just dreaming of it is half the fun.

One question often asked is, "What if, in two or three years, you decide you don't like it? You will have to start all over." In the first place, we are not suggesting that full-time RV living be the end of everything. Not at all—it is a change, from one lifestyle to another as you travel this "only once" road. So we ask, "Start *what* all over? Our lives?"

When we came to the realization that conceivably, we could still live as long as we have already lived, we thought: How many changes have taken place in this first half of our lives? These many changes could still take place! So, while this may not be our lifestyle for another fifty years, we can enjoy it until the time comes (or doesn't) to change again.

If you really think this question through, you'll quickly realize that everything you need for everyday living (linens, dishes, tools, clothing, decorator items, etc.) are already with you in your RV. In fact, this is Deanne's favorite part: Getting to be on a vacation without having forgotten to bring a thing.

All you would need to replace is some furniture, if you should choose to "change" again, and move into a stationary place.

You can sell your RV, if that day comes, and perhaps have enough money to put a down payment on a house. Or you could rent a furnished place in one of your favorite spots. Just imagine: You will have had the blessing of being able to live in the area of your home before moving into it. You will probably inspect it much more thoroughly than most people, who often never even get to choose the place where they live, because they were born there or their jobs required it.

As the old saying goes: "Nothing is permanent except death and taxes." While we are alive we can try to change whatever we want. If you have a dream, don't give up until you've reached for it with all you've got. It is possible, or at least it is a possibility. Trying for it can only be positive. Go for it—you'll never attain it without trying.

2 ───────────────────────────────

YOU MEAN LEAVE THE KIDS, OUR TREASURED THINGS, AND ALL OF OUR FRIENDS?

"For a man's life consisteth not in the
abundance of the things which he possesseth."
Luke 12:15

When we first envisioned a full-timer's life, we had so many questions. Personally, we knew no one who lived such a life, and therefore, had no one to ask questions of. However, there were some good books on the market, and scattered magazine articles written every month in RV-related publications. We devoured them all. Just as we would think we understood the lifestyle, new and better information would be offered for eager people like us.

Finally, we decided to set a date and aim for it. We knew that once we got on the road we would have to take our chances, but also realized that if we didn't just "bite the bullet" we would never go. It is our hope that in sharing all we can about what's ahead for you, we can help you in setting your date.

Everyone Loves Our Sense of Daring— I Think

Most of the rest of society has yet to figure out how people like us live. "Are they part of the homeless masses?" "Are they flighty people—here today, gone tomorrow?" "Can they be trusted not to leave the rest of society holding their bills, responsibilities, and unfinished business?"

Sometimes, as we begin to explain our lives to people with whom we're having only a casual conversation, we see questioning looks on their faces. We know the first few responses will be, "But how do you know where you live? When you go home at night, where do you go?" Then they cautiously look us up and down, trying to determine whether our clothes are ragged or our eyes shifty, as they clutch their purses or wallets a little tighter. They step back a bit—and only then carefully ease back into our circle as we give them the "right" answers.

It is amusing—but very understandable. After all, the average person may never have even heard of such a thing (except perhaps through Charles Kuralt, who got paid for his adventures) much less ever having met someone who does it. But if we give them time—if we have their attention for fifteen minutes—they usually go away with a smile and a spring in their step. "What? You mean we don't have to live life like our parents and our grandparents?" Or: "There really is life after retirement, one where there's not even room for a porch—let alone a rocking chair? Wait 'til I tell Henry!"

What Do You Give Up?

Your House

In our case, we made the decision to sell our home, because it was too large for us once the kids had gone anyway. But it isn't absolutely necessary, or sometimes it is not even desirable, that you give up your stationary home—especially if you will be partial full-timers.

Some advantages of selling your home are:

- You can live on the funds from the sale of your home.

- You don't have to worry about renters taking care of your home, or be concerned about returning to it to place new ads and/or make it ready for the next occupants in case of vacancy.

- If some of your family or friends live in your home, it may cause unnecessarily strained relationships if they don't care for it as you would.

- If you choose to leave your home unoccupied so that you can return to it any time, you must consider ongoing maintenance, yard care, payments, and taxes.

- You must return to winterize it, and make sure necessary repairs are kept up-to-date—and regularly check on its security from pests and vandals.

Returning to our home upon its demand was one main reason we chose to sell. If we were enjoying the autumn colors of the east coast, we didn't want to have to pack up and make an expensive trip back to California if we got a call that our house was to be vacated within thirty days.

We feel that some reasons for keeping your home would be:

- If you really wanted to return to "terra firma" once in a while.

- If you couldn't bear to part with some things that don't fit in your RV (which you don't want to entrust to anyone else.)

- Property values keep rising in your hometown, and you like the security of having a ready-made place to go (one you can afford) if and when the time comes.

Our comment to you is this: If you have any doubts about this lifestyle, hold onto your home for a few years, or at least until you feel you are ready to make a decision about it. Just remember Thomas Wolfe's statement: "You can't go home again."

Caution

> *The "Rule of 55" is the one-time capital gains exemption if you are over the age of 55 when you sell your home, and do not plan to reinvest the capital gains into a home of equal or greater value. It only applies to those who qualify. Contact your accountant before you make the decision about selling or not selling your home.*

Your Things

One worry we had to face when deciding whether to full-time or not was what to do with things that we loved: Deanne's mother's teapot, Gene's favorite books and familiar tools, our grandfather clock, china, and pictures. They were, without a doubt, valuable to us (even if to no one else) but we made a decision about these items based on two considerations:

• If we lived our lives for things—which we couldn't take with us anyway, or wouldn't even have in case of theft, fire, flood or other natural disaster—we had it backwards. Time, and our lives, were the most important things we possessed. We wanted to live whatever we had of them to their utmost. We had reached the age where we realized that life is fleeting—and it is fleeting ever faster every day. We didn't want to get hung up on *things*.

• In looking at treasures we loved, we knew that there were also people we loved even more so we put the two together: We took advantage of dividing up our "spoils" ourselves.

*Precious keepsakes can be passed on
and still enjoyed on visits.*

Our children had individual desires for certain items and we made sure they got them before they obtained them as a result of our Last Wills and Testaments. Special friends, whom we would see more often now because they had lived far away from California, were to receive beloved books, clocks, and pictures. In short, we could still enjoy our things by getting to share the joy they brought to people we loved, when we visited. Another great blessing is knowing they now maintain them for us.

Your Children/Grandchildren

Deanne admits that this is the most heartrending part of our lifestyle. Just as most parents and grandparents will understand, to turn loose of those parent/child relationships that have now become good friendships is hard. Letting go of those tiny grandchildren's hands that entwine in yours, now that you're free to spend time at the playgrounds and rocking them to sleep, is not easy. Again, several important realizations helped us with our decision here:

- It is good for us not to live too close to them. We can spend quality time with our family now that we're not so close that we see every shortcoming in their lives. Besides, now we know that we can come to visit anytime, with no danger of them coming back home to live!

- Most people stay in one place in order to be near the kids. We determined that once our children were grown and married, we couldn't rely on their always living where we were anyway. If their jobs required a move to a distant city, they would go without asking us. And rightly so.

- With children living in different parts of the country anyway, we would get to see each of them more often, and stay as long as we liked—in our own home.

- With today's travel as fast as it is, we would always be close enough to come back in an emergency. We could even close the motorhome and fly to them for a visit if we wished. Not only that, but if we wanted to have some of our family come to visit us, they could just as easily fly our way.

Your Friends

We had many friends we hated to leave, but the truth is, we see them as often now as we did when we were busy working and lived in the same town. While parting brought some tears, our friendships have become more valuable because of the interesting things we talk about when we see each other again.

We now see much more of the friends who do not live in California. Because we're on the road, we can go to visit them much more often. No, we didn't lose our friends. We gained deeper friendships—that stand the test of time and space.

Your Space

We occasionally admit to being a little envious of space enough to entertain more than two guests at once. However, we now entertain around a campfire—or when it is too cold (and it is our turn) we share in a restaurant that the residents in that area are happy to recommend.

Deanne admits that she would like more room to set up an exercise area (although Gene smiles and says she wouldn't use it anyway). The tradeoff has been the joy of being able to ride our bikes in new and different settings (and up higher hills—ugh).

If your RV is arranged for full-timing, privacy is not a problem. Most have a separate bedroom with a door that closes. Often Gene opts for the bedroom, or out under a tree, for watching or listening to a ballgame—or Deanne uses the bedroom for quiet reading. As we write this book, we sometimes use our second, small computer set up on the picnic table outside the motorhome. It's much like the joys of schooldays when classes were taken out on the lawn when warm weather allowed.

Your Routine

While the routine of Friday night poker games or get-togethers with old friends will go by the wayside, think of the new experiences you will enjoy. Campgrounds usually provide nondenominational church services, pot-lucks, square dancing, card games, Bingo, tournaments of different kinds, costume parades, or craft shows. Get involved! You'll meet new people, and enjoy many different types of entertainment, without feeling that your life is in a rut.

When you return to visit your hometown friends, you can get together for that Friday night get-together anyway, with new and exciting things to share. Maybe the introvert you were when you left "home" will have naturally emerged into a person who attracts listeners easily.

Deanne does miss the ability to be involved in particular community events that can sometimes last over a period of months. For instance, she has expressed the desire to help with our high school class reunions, which take a year of planning and working. She also wishes she could finish her last class in Handsigning for the Deaf, which would take a trimester, but would complete her certificate. Our lifestyle allows us to stay in a given area for any length of time we desire. However, our longing to travel always seems to outweigh our yearning to stay in one place long enough to complete such endeavors.

What Do You Gain?

Your House

Have you ever traveled throughout our beautiful country, and expressed a desire to live in every picturesque home you saw? It could have been sprawling farmland, a large mansion with spacious lawns, lovely townhouses beside the beach, or just neighborhoods that show suburban living at its finest—schools and parks included. Then you can smile and admit that you can't live in all of them. No one can.

Our house—complete with garage!

Well, your new home will be just one of another kind. While we both confess we have wistful feelings when we see our old home in California, we agree that it is getting its full use. It is now owned by a family who needs the room and the facilities of a family home. We were through with it, and needed smaller quarters anyway. When he feels wistful, Gene remembers the chores that kept him home on the weekends, and is glad that others have their weekends tied down.

We really believe that the longing we feel is not to *live* in our old home again. It's just nostalgia for the good times we had there when our children were growing up.

Now our motorhome is just another kind of American home that others look at and say, "That would be nice." It's our choice—someday we may choose a different home, but we can only live in one house at a time. We love this one—and if we ever have a conversation where we speak of living in any other home, Deanne confesses that she feels a lump in her throat. We have not given up our home; we have changed houses.

Your Things

Gene expressed often, when we lived in our stationary home, that we needed to do a good, general housecleaning—and get rid of some junk. It was always something we would do tomorrow, because there was no need to tackle such a big chore today (we hoped).

But the day came when we had to face the mountains of stuff we had accumulated. We began by selecting those items we wanted to keep; these we put into our motorhome so we had the best of all our things with us when we drove away. Everything that didn't go to family and friends went to garage sales. These lasted seven weeks, and netted us about $9,000. While we held the garage sales, we allowed our children and friends to come and look. If they found things they had given us, or didn't want to see sold, we told them to take those items. The remainder went to the needy, and became a tax write-off.

All we have in storage now are some boxes containing a

lifetime of precious photo albums, necessary tax papers and business paperwork. Our attitude about storage is: If it's in storage, you can't use it anyway. Let someone else enjoy it instead of letting it just rot away. Your perspective may be different. Think carefully.

Rarely have we found we sold something that we wished we still had. Sometimes we still do without them, and sometimes we've had to replace them. One that comes to mind is the pump pot for coffee. Deanne felt that it would not be necessary to have one anymore because the "real" coffee pot would always be with us. However, we found while we were on the road that drinking what we wanted for breakfast left half a pot that would become cold. So we bought another pump pot, and keep it up front for the coffee we want later in the morning as we travel.

We also kept some things that we later decided we didn't need. Bulky tools that we'll probably never use again have gone on to other sales. We have too many blankets—and still too many clothes. Just as it was when we were stationary—we still collect too much junk. Just on a smaller scale.

One thing you might find helpful: If you want to buy a souvenir in a place you visit, buy something useful. A hot pad, mixing bowl, scarf, or new pair of jeans will be used more, seen more, and do more than just gathering dust as a knickknack or picture (for which you won't have room anyway).

Your Children/Grandchildren

Both of us believe our quality time with our children and grandchildren has helped all of us. No longer do we have children who look to us for "advice" on money matters (i.e., a hand-out)—or as convenient babysitters when we might have other plans. We love the time we now have with them, and are happy to spend many hours with the grandchildren, freeing up their parents when we are free. Giving them advice on money matters is now more of a gift than an obligation. Besides, we no longer have the paycheck that allows us to act as a bank, so it truly is a joy to give it when we have it.

Another thought about children/grandchildren that we hadn't expected: As we have gotten closer to faraway friends, and gained good friendships with new ones, we have gotten to know their kids and grandkids.

For instance, we met Max and Fanny, people who winter in Arizona and return to their stationary home in Michigan for the summer. We have become close friends, and now we're with them (and some of our family) while wintering in Arizona. Then we join them and their family when we go north for the summer.

It is amazing how small the world has gotten! These people now all know each other, and we have developed one circle of friends that extends from Michigan to Florida to Arizona to California. Everyone is now interlinked and keeps in touch with one another.

We have expanded our family to include the families of many others. Deanne shudders to think of all the children who call her "Grandma" at such a young age. It is truly a blessing to have such a big "family."

Your Friends

It's true: We have gained many more friends since we have been on the road. They are friends who are just as close to us as those we grew up with at home. It isn't necessarily a fact that you only see every new person just a short time. Sometimes we've developed lasting friendships by being next to someone in a campground for even a day, and then meeting them later in a predetermined place.

Your Space

One of the most ironic questions asked of us is, "Do you just camp all the time?" We laugh, because we can imagine people think we have a countertop that becomes a bed at night, or a bathroom that becomes a shower as needed. No, our home is much like a small apartment. It has all the amenities of a home, only within a smaller space. And it moves when you hear a hurricane is coming!

When we talk about "camping," we mean taking things out of our motorhome and going out someplace to camp.

Sometimes people ask us, "Don't you feel cramped in there?" Our answer: If we do, we go outside. We have modified our motorhome so we do not feel cramped. Because we still run a ministry/business, we've removed our extra chairs and replaced them with a desk and computer. Our tabletop has been replaced with a larger one. We've added shelves to offer more comfortable enjoyment of a cup of coffee on the couch. These are a few of the suggestions that everyone will do to make their RV a home.

Shelves conveniently placed can make your RV homey.

In truth, the joy of living as we do is to appreciate both the inside and outside of our home, with new surroundings every day. As Gene says, "If the grass grows, you don't have to mow it, you can just move."

Someone asked Deanne once if she felt the security of a place to call her own was gone. She thought about that and replied,

"No, if I want my own things, I shut the door. That kind of security still exists; it's inside."

Your Routine

Making yourself a part of any community you visit goes a long way toward finding more routine than you may even want. Deanne presents free-will offering song concerts in churches throughout the U.S. and Canada. When we're in a town for more than one night, the first thing we do is seek out churches and attend services. We find that more often than not, we are welcomed to all kinds of church activities, and are invited to many people's homes for fellowship. This not only builds friendships, but if we're not careful, we find ourselves getting back into a routine and wanting to stay there (and everywhere else). Just as, when we look at all the different homes throughout America, we want to live in all of them.

We have also found that if a campground we're in does not provide activities, going to the local Chamber of Commerce, reading the local newspaper, or just taking a jaunt downtown to talk with the locals will provide all the routine happenings we can handle.

In a nutshell—and to use an old cliche—"Today is the first day of the rest of your life." Live it as if it were your last.

3

How Can We Afford
Such a Lifestyle?

*"For which of you, intending to build a tower, sitteth
not down first, and counteth the cost, whether he have
sufficient to finish it?"* **Luke 14:28**

We had decided to live our full-time RV life several years before
we "folded up our tent and stole off into the night." In fact, we
had planned to wait until we retired to go.

In reality, then, when we finally drove out of California on
our quest for "a higher calling," it was done long before we had
planned to do so. But—*don't overlook this word of caution: We
did not do so without counting the costs.*

The books we had read, and our plans for working at stationary jobs until retirement—and then using our retirement funds to
live "forever," from "sea to shining sea"—had to be rethought
and replaced with creative ideas that would allow us to "leave
home" while we were still young. We would have to support
ourselves, we knew, for another fifteen years before we would be
of retirement age, so we had to take a hard look at how that
would work for us.

It was on this subject that we found no help. Books written on
full-timing seemed to cover retirement-age work that earned
stipends and a free campground hookup. That world consisted of
completely leaving behind the busy, work-a-day clamor and

headaches, and trading it for "fun work" in a holiday environment. Our employment would have to combine income-earning work with vacation: We would get to see America while we traveled, and stay in places where the atmosphere shouted, "VACATION" But we would still have to be part of the working world if we were to earn enough money to support ourselves.

Would the joy of seeing the country, living in a free-and-easy environment, offset the fact that we had to continue to work hard? Would we be free of "the rat-race headaches"? Since we had no books to refer to, we were to find out through trial and error.

In this chapter, we will address ideas for those of you who, like us, want to leave before "your time." We will be honest about what you will find. We will share some hints on what we have found, sometimes the hard way, so that maybe you can be even better prepared than we were. Then, once you "hit the road," you will not be forced to "go home again"—at least not for lack of knowledge.

How We Did It

Let us start by telling you how we came around to the day we decided: "This is the day—not in ten or fifteen years—Today!"

In 1987, our last child got married, and we were left with the empty nest syndrome. We took a few months to enjoy the quiet of our now too-large home and get back into the throes of running our own business (a technical writing service for California clients) without having to care for a family. Suddenly the light dawned: We were now free to do whatever we wanted for the rest of our lives.

This revelation first came from our discussion whether to sell our home and buy a smaller, no-yard condo or apartment. After all, if we were going to move anyway, why bother with having to create another home, when we had a perfectly good "home" sitting in our driveway. One we had already chosen and purchased. We could live in it—now!

We talked about where we would like to go (everywhere). What we would like to pay (as little as possible). With so much to choose from, which location would our work require us to select? We decided we could expand our writing horizons and take the whole country.

Although Gene held a nine-to-five engineering job while writing on the side, Deanne worked the business full-time. One day, she began to think about what else she might like to do besides writing, now that she was free from family constraints. Singing has always been her first love, and although she had only sung in local churches, she now thought about singing in many churches. She could fulfill her lifelong dream of ministering to many others, and maybe even earn an income presenting full concerts.

That opened Pandora's Box. The creative juices began to flow. What else did Gene want to do? He is an engineer, so he knows how to design things, manufacture them, and show others how to do what he has done.

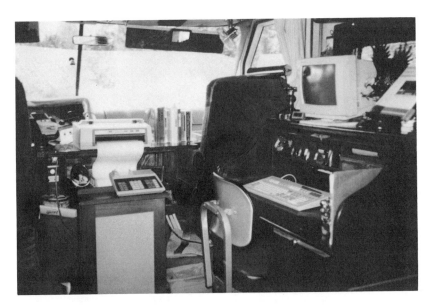

We take along our rolltop desk and computer.

We could write newspaper and RV magazine articles on maintaining and upgrading RVs, and Gene could even help others around the campgrounds. We could expand our technical writing services to include our own RV book, and even hold seminars, where we could share with others what they can do to make their full-time RV life more exciting.

Would that do it? What else could we do? We could continue to work in our business on a national (or even worldwide) basis, if we wanted. Our computer could be installed in the roll-top desk in our living room, and we could write as we traveled. With the correct telephone setup, California clients could still reach us, and we could return there to do technical writing as needed.

What is our point? Start with what you know, then add what you would like to do and what it would take to do it. Decide whether it would fit into this lifestyle, then build outward.

It was scary. Although we had already decided that living in an RV was what we wanted to do, it was a huge step from knowing that the day was coming, to putting the house up for sale. But as Deanne thought about it (without telling Gene, because, as he admits, he would have said yes in only about ten seconds, compared to her long decision time) it began to make sense.

Our house was put on the market, our things were packed into the motorhome, given away, and sold as we emptied the house in readiness. Then, on the last day of August 1987, we pulled away from our former, stationary address and into our new one, and the whole of America became our home.

Planning for Your Dream

There were several things that were very important in preparing for, and working in, our new world. They will be equally important for you:

1. Planning/Saving for Your Dream—Investing
2. Membership Campgrounds—Are They Worth the Cost?
3. Making Money While You Travel
4. What Trades Are Amenable to Travel?
5. Budgeting

Planning/Saving for Your Dream—Investing

One very important caution we read when starting our business in 1981 holds true for starting a working life as a full-timer: Have enough money put aside so that you can live for the first six months until the funds begin coming in.

You may leave your stationary home with your job/business already in progress, which we believe is the best idea, if you can do it. However, there still will be expenses you did not have (when your home did not move) which you probably will not expect as you begin this new life. Don't start out by using your credit cards to get you on your way; *Save.*

It is important that you put money away while working your "stationary" jobs. As we all know, this is not easy. Perhaps your job allows you to put part of your paycheck into an account, or your company is building a retirement fund for you. Each of us has a different situation, and each a different way of saving, but there are many plans to choose from.

Several years before we left, we refinanced our home, and using our home's equity, bought five other houses. These were houses that we rented out, and thus they bring us income while we are on the road.

We also purchased stock in mutual funds. This allowed us to distribute our money over a large stock base, and have someone else manage it. Our eggs were not all in one basket, so we didn't have to worry that if one stock fell, we would lose all our savings. Certificates of deposit, money market, and passbook savings accounts are only a small sample of the viable places to save money, and you should discuss with your accountant or broker the best place for you to put yours.

Owning our own business, we didn't have a retirement plan building for us. We invested in Keough plans and IRAs up to the maximum we could afford. Therefore, when we do reach retirement age, we'll be prepared to go on with our lifestyle.

New Priorities

A change of attitude also occurred during this five-year planning stage, regarding the purchase of anything that would not fit into our motorhome. For instance, if the washing machine broke, it was repaired instead of replaced, because it would not fit into our future. It would have to be sold. Gene wanted to replace his eleven-year-old motorcycle, but a motorcycle was not part of what we planned to take. The old one stayed with us until the end. The same was true for TV sets, all home appliances, and yard or garden tools.

The point here is that we started this planning stage about five years before we left. We had planned to save several years more before we departed, but five years' savings was better than none.

Membership Campgrounds—Are They Worth the Cost?

As a family, we had been camping for twenty-plus years. To avoid the crowded camping conditions in Southern California, we had already purchased a "home park membership." To be a weekend camper in Southern California, one often has to plan months in advance for a simple reservation, and our schedule only permitted spur-of-the-moment trips. Our campground membership allowed us that freedom.

This purchase also included membership in Camp Coast-to-Coast, a reciprocal camping organization. We had used our home park regularly for weekend camping trips. However, we had never taken advantage of our ability to stay in other campgrounds for one dollar a night—until after we left home. It was then that we came to appreciate our foresight in having joined Coast-to-Coast.

We had also joined Thousand Trails (later adding NACO and Resort Parks International (RPI) after we were on the road). Thousand Trails permits you to stay in their parks without charge provided your annual dues are paid, for a specified time period. So as we travel we stay the allotted number of weeks in a given campground (hopefully Thousand Trails or NACO since they're free) and stay the "out" period in a nearby Coast-to-Coast or RPI park.

Recently we purchased a membership in Thousand Adventures, Inc. (TAI). This adds to our basic number of membership parks where we pay no daily rates (only our annual dues, which sustain the parks and our privilege of using them). Our basic reason for this purchase was that there are now forty-eight parks within TAI, which are mostly east of the Mississippi, and more are constantly added. This allows us more freedom in selecting where we can minister and spend longer blocks of time (up to twenty-one days in each of the forty-eight parks). Another reason for this purchase was that TAI incurs no debt against purchased parks, thus assuring TAI members solvency of their purchase in a very volatile market.

We now have access to more than seven hundred campgrounds across the U.S., Canada, and Mexico. The value has been well worth the original cost to us. However, we have met people who feel that the high pressure sales tactics of membership campgrounds (and the bankruptcies of some of them) make it a scary proposition to spend four to nine thousand dollars to join, when it may not be a necessity.

It's true that for some, membership campgrounds are not necessary. For instance, the people who work in campgrounds for their income also generally earn their monthly camping fee. Those who only travel several months a year can earn enough money in their "stationary" months to pay the ten to forty dollars a night to stay in public campgrounds. People who love boondocking (staying in the desert, mountains, or somewhere beside a beautiful stream) may not be interested in being part of a membership organization.

We say: Good for them. The name of the game is: Do what you want to do. For us, membership campgrounds are a necessity because we need the power hookup for our computer at least part of the time. And we don't regret having bought them. We live in the system, and the free stay, or one to two dollars per night charge, greatly offsets the yearly dues that we would spend in a few weeks if we had to pay per night.

Following are some pros and cons of membership:

Pros

1. Membership campgrounds are usually cleaner than public ones, and their security systems are, for the most part, good.

2. You rarely have problems getting into a membership campground without reservations. Exceptions to this are on holidays, Friday night or Saturday check-in, or when using the more popular parks. ("Popular" parks will let you know of their reservation policies in the monthly magazines that you receive when you belong to that member organization.)

3. Belonging to membership campgrounds has other benefits beyond using their camping facilities. Tour packages, cruises, group life insurance, airplane and rental car rate discounts, rallies, and so on, are worthwhile advantages when you are on the road.

4. A recent development in the membership campground market has been the resale organizations. They have made available greatly discounted memberships on most of the parks around the U.S. People who, for various reasons, must sell their memberships, put them on consignment with these organizations.

Caution

> Be cautious of any resale organization requir-
> ing up-front fees in order to be added to their
> list of memberships for sale. Most legitimate
> resale organizations will list your membership
> with the fee to be collected at the time of sale.

5. You may find campground memberships listed for sale by
   individuals at greatly reduced prices in the Classified sections
   of most RV magazines and news publications. Check them
   out; the discount may be worth giving up the "free gift" for
   a brand new membership.

Cons

1. Bankruptcies (or Chapter 11s) of a membership campground
   are definitely fears that have been realized over the years
   since membership campgrounds have been introduced. Check
   into the history of a membership organization, and talk to
   people who already belong to it. Nothing is absolute, but
   through good research you should be confident of the proba-
   bility of your organization's staying-power. Bankruptcies will
   leave you with only a court date for your money.

2. An unclean or sloppily-run park is subject to ousting from its
   membership organization. Be sure to investigate the park
   yourself; ask other members about its reputation. Call the
   membership organization to find out if the park is in good
   standing with them. If that organization ever withdraws your
   home park from their system for any breach of contract, your
   membership in RPI, Coast-to-Coast, etc., may go with it.

Comments

1. Some membership camping organizations have a 125-mile
   radius rule, which says that you can't use any reciprocal

campground within 125 miles of your home park. Therefore, when choosing a home park, purchase a membership in one that is not close to any other park you might wish to use. For example: Our children are in Southern California. When we go to see them, we can only stay in our own Coast-to-Coast home park, or pay a high monthly fee to go into Orange County and stay in a public RV park. Although we can stay in our home park for thirty days at a time, it is ninety miles from Orange County. Our other membership parks such as NACO, Thousand Trails, and RPI are an equal distance from Orange County, so it's either money spent for gas, or money spent for an RV space. We usually opt for the RV space.

An alternative to this situation might be to purchase an additional home park that is far away from anyone you know. Then the 125-mile rule will not affect any park in which you choose to stay. Request that this new park be named as your home park when joining RPI or Camp Coast-to-Coast. We would not suggest buying this other park at new prices. Watch for someone selling their membership in a magazine or resale organization. The reduced price will offset the fact that you may not be able to resell that park quite as readily as if you bought new.

2. If you choose to buy into a membership campground, do so before you leave your stationary job if you are going to make monthly payments on it, so that you can qualify for the loan. Even better, if you can, pay for it before you leave so that you won't have to meet those high monthly payments.

   Remember, even if you don't use your reciprocal membership privileges before you leave, they will prove to be of great value later.

We have met several people who have expressed frustration with us for using our membership campgrounds full-time. Their reasoning is that they paid the same membership fee as we did, and they only get to use the park(s) a few times a year—their jobs and other responsibilities precluding their use more often. They maintain that for that same price, we virtually have free rent and utilities year-round. We don't argue, but wonder if they're not a little envious. We all agreed to the same price, to use the system in our own way. We don't have a corner on the market for our park(s)' full time use. They can join us any time. If they don't want to, or can't, that's something they will want to work out to fit their own dreams.

In addressing this situation with managers of the various parks, we have been told that in the off-season, full-timers are generally the reason why these parks are even kept open, with full security and staffing—thus affording everyone an open park with experienced personnel year-round.

RV and Travel Clubs

Camping clubs such as Good Sam, Escapees (SKP's), Family Motor Coach Association, and various clubs formed for individual brand-name RV owners are all worth looking into. They offer benefits such as cruises, tours, rallies, and discounts, as well as friendships with others like us who are here to help each other. Their yearly dues are usually very reasonable, and they can give you the stability you may miss when you leave your stationary home (Check Appendix A for a list of many of these RV and travel clubs).

Making Money While You Travel

What Trades are Amenable to Travel?

If we had only one piece of advice to give you about earning a serious income while you travel, it would be this: Be creative! It is now possible for you to do many types of work that you could never have considered before.

Conversely, your regular paycheck may stop, so you will have to figure out how to bring enough money into your home to keep going. Don't limit yourself to trades your parents (peers, teachers) always told you were safe. Create!

As we said, we began by thinking of all the things we've ever wanted to do. There were no limits, because we still may never do them—but we listed them anyway.

For instance, Gene has always wanted to be the pastor of a church, and he put that on his list. In reviewing the list, he realized that he probably would never return to college to get that education now, though earning an income for reading and studying (which he loves to do anyway) was part of the reason to pastor.

So how could he fulfill that dream? He decided that he could use his writing skills to help pastors compose their books. In that way he could still learn while he helped them.

Craftwork is a popular income-maker on the road.

Make your list, and put no limits on it. Maybe you've always wanted to be an Olympic swimmer. You may cross it off in the end—or you may find that traveling will finally give you the opportunity to be close to your subject. Maybe you'll make it yet—or if not, maybe you'll at least have the chance to go wherever the Olympics are being held, and work at some task that makes you part of this special event.

Make your dream list *long*. Make it so long that you won't possibly have time to do it all. Then, as you discuss it with your spouse/friends, and research the possibilities, your list will be fine-tuned into something that is reasonable. Starting by dreaming big may help you see surprising occupations that you will now have the opportunity to try.

Search out the vocations available for your type of life. Ask your librarian to help you find books that list your special kind of work and its related fields; for instance, jobs that require you to work outside, jobs in the glamour field, or jobs that require travel or staying at a specific site for several months.

A good resource is also *Workamper News*, a bimonthly newsletter that advertises jobs specifically for people like us. They have a resume referral service, which boasts a 90%-plus referral record. You can also list work you may be specifically seeking under their "Situations Wanted" column, which is free for the first fifty words. The *National Parks Trade Journal* is a publication that lists over 100,000 jobs suited for living and working in the wilderness. Call or write them; these publications are well worth the price (see Appendix D).

To aid you further, following is a list of vocations you might consider which are amenable to travel. It is only a sample. Use it to work outward into possibilities for you. Keep in mind that some of these jobs may require that you remain in one area for a while. If constant travel is your dream, you will have to take that into account. Our work (concerts, seminars, RV shows and writing) requires that we continually move, but that is the work we've chosen. It outweighs Deanne's desires to be involved in community activities.

Jobs for your Consideration

Actors and Actresses
Antique Dealers
Archaeologists
Arts and Craftspeople
Bakers
Camp Counselors
Campground Hosts
Circus, Carnival, Rodeo
Circuit Workers
Computer Operators
Construction Workers
Cooks
Delivery People
Drivers (for RV delivery)
Evangelists
Financial Advisors
Fishers
Flea Market Concessionaires
Forest Fire Fighters
Forestry Technicians
Fruit and Vegetable
Field Workers
Geologists
Groundskeepers/Gardeners
Housekeepers
Information Booth Workers
Instructors in Various Outdoor
    Sports (Skiing, Golf)
Landscapers
Linemen
Loggers
Motel/Mobile Park Managers
Nannies
Office Managers and
Registration Clerks

Advertising/Promotions (PR)
Anesthesiologists
Artists
Automobile and RV Mechanics
Bookkeepers
Camp Security Workers
Christmas Tree Harvesters
College Recruiters
Civil Engineers
Concessionaires (Marinas, gift
    shops, riding stables)
Craft Instructors
Directors
Electricians
Film Editors
Fire Tower Lookouts
Fishing or Hunting Guides
Food Service Workers
Forest Rangers
Free-Lance News Reporters
Fur Trappers
Gas Station Attendants
Golf Course Groomers
Heavy Duty Equipment
Operators
Inside/Outside Maintenance
    Workers
Interpreters
Lecturers
Livestock Tenders (Cowboys)
Mechanics
Musicians/Singers
Nurses
Oil Field Workers
Party Plan Directors

Pet Sitters	Petroleum or Mining Engineers
Photographers	Pro Golfers, Bowlers, etc.
Proofreaders	Property Watchers (Sitters)
Ranchhands	Recreation Directors
Repair People	Resort Workers
Rodeo Riders	RV Salespeople
RV Parts Supplies Work	"Sambassadors" for Good Sam
Screenwriters	Club
SCUBA Divers	Seamstresses, Tailors
Secretaries	Self-Employment (How about
Stagehands	doing taxes for people like our-
Store Clerks	selves? Or selling a product you
Surveyors	believe in?)
Teachers	Test Drivers (RVs)
Telemarketers	Tram Drivers
Tour Guides	Translators
Tree Surgeons	Typists
Wagonmasters	Welders
Well Drillers	Wildife Biologists
Wildlife Managers	Word Processors
Writers	

Work Awhile/Travel Awhile

Temporary Agencies. We have found that temporary agencies, located around the U.S., are a boon for people like us. When we're near a city for a few weeks, and Deanne finds she has extra time, she has used such agencies to find short-term work as a Word Processor, Secretary, Receptionist, Telemarketer, Proofreader, or Customer Service Representative.

Other temporary jobs are available in industry. These include electronic assembly, welders, shipping/receiving clerks, or production workers. Agencies also request computer programmers and operators and account managers. Don't limit yourself. It doesn't hurt to call the local agencies and ask for any kind of work you do.

The pay is usually better for "temps" than for permanent employees, because the client company doesn't have to pay for fringe benefits. So spruce up your resume and have it handy.

Volunteer Work. Working as a volunteer in a field you particularly like is also a way of making yourself known. When paid positions arise there, you are a viable, proven candidate. Not to mention how good it makes you feel to have helped someone along the way.

If you are blessed with not needing an income, there is a wonderful program for Campground Hosting through the Good Sam Club. These positions usually allow you to park your RV in that particular campground free-of-charge, and the chance to meet and enjoy the camaraderie of others like us is phenomenal. Contact Good Sam and get on their list so that you can choose the area and park in which you would like to help.

Sharing Skills. The most wonderful trait of RV travellers is their friendliness. We feel this is because they are away from home, and they can relax and enjoy life as it was meant to be. It seems that one never lacks help in any type of adversity. People will see each other changing a tire or trying to park their RV, and they naturally want to help. Deanne wonders if it's because we feel useless when we are not being prevailed upon to keep our noses to the grindstone.

We have also found that not only are RV dwellers themselves friendly, but occasionally you meet someone in the RV industry who has such a love for RV living that he feels akin to our lifestyle. At Christmas in 1990, we found one such person, and we want to take the time to commend him, and recommend his business to you:

We had met a man in a campground in Anaheim, California, who had serious health problems. His medical costs overrode his need for something other than the shabby curtains he had hanging in his RV. We drove to Garden Grove, and asked the owner of an RV service company if he had any leftover curtains, from a remodeling job, that he was going to throw away. We offered to hang the curtains if the owner would donate them. No curtains were available, but he had a stack of new and used venetian blinds that he let us poke through until we found the right sizes for the job.

All told, we got several hundred dollars worth of blinds—and this man's time to help us uncover them. We recommend this RV repair facility to you, if you're ever in Southern California: California Coachworks, 11801 Westminster Ave, Garden Grove, CA 92643, (714) 554-9001. The owner's name is Blair McCullogh. Tell him we sent you. He'll remember; he's one of us.

People do all sorts of hobbies on the road. Finding someone with a sewing machine, blender, microwave, or something that one may not normally bring with them in their RV is easy. Just ask. Everyone seems to love helping.

Some folks with hobbies such as cooking, baking, sewing, painting, or craftwork naturally find their niche when it comes to making extra income. Fresh doughnuts baked and sold to campground guests are so welcome with a cup of coffee and a sit in the sunshine on a Saturday morning. Although we generally don't have room for any paintings we can buy directly from an artist, it's fun to buy them for a friend or relative. We then have the joy of giving them a personally autographed painting from a place they may never get to visit.

In one campground, Gene spotted a man who had just bought a fifth-wheel, fresh off the showroom floor. He was so excited that when the dealer hooked his rig up to his truck and waved him off down the road, the man forgot to ask him how they did it. Getting to the campground and unhooking was easy. Gene came upon him on his way to the shower one morning. The man was trying to hook back up to leave the campground, and looked like he was about to cry. The shower waited while Gene showed him how it worked.

It's a good thing we're a helpful bunch. Most of us are so excited when coming out that we don't stop to listen when told about how we are going to keep ourselves on the road—much less ask for such information when it is not offered.

It was so gratifying to see the look on that man's face. Evidently RV traveling was new to him, because he seemed so surprised to find free help or assistance that didn't cost him an arm and a leg.

Parking Until the Funds Catch Up. While we were saving for our full-timing life, there came a gas crunch, and many RVs were being sold for little or nothing. People thought if they couldn't afford gas for their automobiles, they surely weren't going to waste it on a leisure wagon.

Thus, that line of thinking prevailed, and when we bought our RV, our friends asked incredulously, "How many miles to the gallon does that thing get?" When Gene answered, "Four or five," they stammered, "That's not very good, is it?" His reply: "Well, it's not too good for a car, but it's not too bad for a house!"

If you add up what you would pay to travel across country in a car, having to allow for meals eaten out, motels, and so on, compared to the money spent on the RV's low miles-per-gallon it would probably equal that which is saved by getting to stay in your own rig and cook your own meals.

We still have people ask us how we can afford to keep our motorhome on the road. It is true that it costs about seven hundred dollars for us to drive, say, from California to Florida. However, you don't have to keep moving your RV as though the police will give you a ticket if you stop.

You can stop for months at a time if you like. Some people will take advantage of "coyote camping" or "boondocking" while waiting for funds to catch up. It gives them a chance to enjoy the other half of full-time RV-ing: Roughing it.

It is also relatively cheap to stay in a campground, even the ones that are not membership owned, compared to most hotels or motels. Sometimes campgrounds have much reduced monthly rates. Thus, parking your RV until you have money again gives one a chance to see a given area for a longer time. It's all in how you look at it. We prefer to look at it positively.

Budgeting

Just as budgeting is a necessity in a stationary home, it will be a lifesaver when you're on the road. Without a budget, the temptation to buy from all the vacation spots you will visit (not as a vacationer, remember) may be overwhelming. The opportunities to overspend on all the different foods, clothes, and cultural memorabilia may leave you with "culture shock."

Following is a sample budget that you probably can use. Of course, this budget is merely a guideline. You'll want to raise or lower, and add or subtract items to suit your family. Just don't forget to consider each item; they will probably appear in every full-timer's budget in some way or another.

The only item in the budget that we have found out of proportion is the $50/month for RV maintenance. We have spent well over that amount (Deanne says we're up to the year 2000 in that area of the budget). After many years, it is finally beginning to come to a break-even point. It seemed that with a new RV, there was so much to add, make livable, and—much to our chagrin—correct. Many ordinary components in an RV are made of plastic, because they are not designed for continual use, but for occasional camping. We have had to replace faucets, light fixtures, door handles, latches—and on and on—with real parts, from a hardware store, in order for the part to endure as it would have to in a stationary home. We suppose that when we get it all done the way we want it, we'll get bored and want to trade up. After all, we are still Americans!

Typical Budget for Full-Timers

Following are typical amounts put aside each month, to earn interest until the time that each payment is due:

$ 132.50	RV/tow vehicle insurance savings
100.00	Tax Savings
13.00	License Plate Savings
60.00	Membership Campground dues savings
12.50	Misc. other dues/subscriptions savings (AARP, magazines, etc.)
$ 318.00	Sub-Total

These are typical charges for monthly living expenses:

$ 400.00	Gas/Lodging (if you belong to a membership campground)
35.00	LP Gas
175.00	Tithe to church or others to whom you give
50.00	Life Insurance
250.00	Health Insurance
20.00	Banking service charges
200.00	Food
50.00	RV Maintenance
100.00	Personal allowance for fun
35.00	Postal Service charges (mail forwarding, box rental, etc.)
100.00	Telephone message service
25.00	Long-distance telephone charges
40.00	Miscellaneous (stamps, laundry, etc.)
$ 1480.00	Sub-total
$ 1798.00	**Total**

Add any other payments that are individual to all of us, such as RV payments, time payments and/or bank card payments. Include personal supplies such as clothing and shoes, hobby supplies, gifts and routine medical and dental expenses.

Caution

If you leave home before you have fully paid for your RV, it may put a greater strain on you than you can afford and still maintain your lifestyle. Weigh carefully any decision to include such a large monthly payment in your budget. If possible, pay for it ahead of time.

4

HOW WILL PEOPLE KNOW WHERE WE ARE?

"Thou (O Lord) tellest my wanderings . . . "
Psalm 56:8

How Will We Handle . . .

. . . Choosing a Home State?

One big benefit to living the full-time RV life is being able to choose your home state. Think about it. How many gripes and complaints have you got against the state you live in now? Full-timing presents you with the opportunity to change all of that. No state is perfect, but you can enjoy all the good things about the state of your choice, without having to *live* there. For example, we enjoy all the benefits of Florida, but we don't have to live with the bugs, heat, and humidity in the summertime.

You can look at all the pros and cons of each state's taxes (sales, income, property), license plate fees, vehicle insurance rates, fault/no fault insurance laws, driver's license fees/rules, property values, and voting regulations, and you are free to take your choice.

We chose Florida as our home state for several reasons. First, we already owned some property there, which gave us a convenient "real" address. Also, the cost of our motorhome's license plates was *3%* of the price we had paid in California. Additionally, there is no state income tax in Florida, vehicle insurance for that locality is reasonable, no-fault insurance is the law, voting by absentee ballot is allowed, and we could obtain a Florida-only driver's license without having to surrender our California one. That way, when we're in Florida to handle our business, we have a driver's license to do it with. When we're in California, where our children live, we can do our banking without having an out-of-state license. "Besides," Gene says, "a local driver's license may be necessary to rent videos." Now *that's* important.

There are no laws against choosing a state and making it your domicile without having a residence there, and it's relatively easy to choose your home state.

We bought a handbook entitled *Selecting an RV Home Base*, which lists all of the states and each of their requirements for making it your home base. If you obtain this book, be sure to check the publication date, because these laws do change. At the time of this writing, it's still available through Trailer Life Enterprises in Agoura Hills, California, and it helped us immensely.

To assist you even further, we suggest consideration of the following, more popularly chosen states (for the obvious reasons you will probably decide for yourself) when weighing all of the above variables: Oregon, Texas, Florida, Nevada, Idaho, Washington State, and Wyoming.

Our advice in choosing a state is to be honest about following all the rules. Don't try to license your vehicle in one state, and pay taxes in another. We full-timers do have a wonderful benefit, but taking unfair advantage of it can get you into trouble. Beware.

You may still own your home and choose to keep that state as your home state, or you may have good reasons for choosing another, different state. It's your choice. Enjoy! You should choose based on your own circumstances. We suggest you see your accountant and/or an attorney to determine your legal status.

. . . Mail/Periodicals

Most states require that you have a home address, or as they call it, "a physical place of residence" (versus a Post Office Box), to declare it your home state. This will have to do with voting privileges, license plates, driver's licenses, taxes (sales, income, property), vehicle insurance rates, and fault/no fault insurance laws. The first thing you will want to do is find a home address that will allow you to receive your mail (and have it forwarded) in order for the rest of the above considerations to fall in line.

Unless you keep your home and use that address as your permanent address—or own or rent property in the state of your choice—you might think you have no alternative but to obtain or keep your property. This is not true; you have several options:

- You can use the residence of one of your children or a friend—someone who is willing to let you use their address. This was not an option for us, because as much as we love our children, we didn't want to have to change our address every time they changed theirs. Besides, it was possible that our mail might have gotten lost or forgotten on their kitchen counter or desk.

  Some of our friends wanted to help us, but it would have been an imposition to them, for which we would have felt obliged to pay. Thus, since we were going to pay anyway, we chose to handle the situation in a businesslike manner—with someone whose job it would be to meet our postal needs.

- There are private mail receiving services located in every state, which make it their business to receive and forward your mail. These services are usually quite reasonable (about $135/year, plus postage. Second-day, Priority Mail rate of $3.00 for packages up to two pounds makes a very reasonable forwarding rate); and there are four distinct advantages to using this type of service instead of the U.S. Postal Service:

1. The service is personal. Such businesses are usually not so large that you cannot become acquainted with their personnel. Thus, you can drop them a note telling them where you'll be and when. A quick telephone call will make any changes you need, without causing you to feel that you're dealing with The Government. You may want to call someone in this company, and they can tell you if you have a particular letter you might be waiting for in your box. They can then send it Special Delivery.

2. These services maintain a street address, and their boxes may be called "suites" rather than P.O. Boxes. Voila! A secure, permanent home or office address for you. You can feel confident that your mail is safely located in a locked box.

3. UPS delivers to private mail receiving services; they do not deliver to government Post Offices.

4. Typing/word processing, copy and fax machines, packaging and package-forwarding, and Notary Public are some services that may be offered by these establishments.

These places are advertised in many RV magazines in the classified ads. They're also listed in the Yellow Pages under Mail Receiving Services. They're worth looking into for your peace of mind, mail security, and convenience—for a nominal rate.

•   Check with your gas credit card provider, Good Sam, Discover Card, and other membership organizations to which you may belong. Some provide a free mail forwarding service, requiring only that you pay postage.

Your mail can be forwarded to General Delivery, care of the local Post Office where you are temporarily located; to the people you are visiting; or to the campground where you are parked.

Caution

> *Be sure to check with the particular camp-ground office where you plan to stay. Find out if they will accept forwarded mail; some have expressed their rule against this practice. If so, General Delivery may be your alternative.*

You may want to consider stopping subscriptions to all magazines/periodicals that are fairly easy to find on a magazine rack. Rerouting such heavy material can add enough weight to your forwarding charges that it will eliminate any savings you may have had with subscription rates. Perhaps we should all contact publishers of periodicals and magazines, requesting the purchase of coupons instead of direct subscriptions—to be exchanged at magazine racks for the actual product. We may convince them of the necessity for this service to full-timers and others on the road.

How do we do it? We have an arrangement with our mail service company to forward our mail every Friday. We keep them informed, either by telephone or a letter written ahead of time with our schedule on it, about where that mail should arrive. It has been well worth the price.

. . . Telephones?

There are many different ways to handle the making and receiving of your telephone calls when you live on the road:

Standard Telephone Service. Gene has wired our motorhome for a standard telephone in every room—the bedroom, the galley, and the living room. There is also an outlet on the outside of the motorhome, under the awning, to provide a convenient outside telephone jack. Deanne says that she has always lovingly referred to Gene as "The Gadget Man," and she appreciates having so many telephones. It is great not having to walk far to answer any of them.

Whenever we are staying in a friend's driveway, this wiring allows us to be temporarily connected to their telephone service. Thus, if our friends are away for the day, we can help by answering their calls. Also, by using our telephone calling card, we can make any of our own calls from our RV.

You can also make use of standard telephone service from anywhere you may want to call home. It might be a friend's or relative's house, or even a campground where you can have a telephone service connection made during your stay.

Cellular Telephones. Cellular telephone service is growing rapidly throughout the United States. However, because the establishment of cellular service is so costly to service providers, most of the areas covered are, at this time, high density population areas.

Representatives of the industry have assured us that as the percentage of users increases, the areas of coverage must also expand. Based upon past growth figures, our best guess would be that the coverage should warrant our investment in a cellular telephone in two or three more years.

At the time of this writing, however, unless you spend most of your time in and around the larger metropolitan areas of the nation, you will probably be disappointed with cellular telephone use, and equally astonished at the monthly cost.

We must say that if you decide to use this service—while it is relatively expensive—it has some very good features (many of them features of the telephone set itself, and some are features of a particular cellular service):

• Automatic signal level control (in a given service area), which assures signal clarity.

• Your security—while on the road (within a service area) you can make emergency calls without leaving your vehicle.

- "Roaming feature," which allows you to use your cellular telephone in other service areas.

- "Call forwarding" to your cellular telephone. If you maintain a stationary home or office that has the call forwarding service, your calls can be automatically forwarded to you wherever you are.

- "Call waiting," which announces an incoming call while you are making or taking another telephone call.

- The "no-answer transfer feature" will allow any calls to the cellular telephone to be forwarded to you, wherever you are.

- Portability—some cellular telephones can be carried in your briefcase or even your pocket.

- "Conferencing feature" can be activated to allow you to talk to more than one party at a time.

- Speed dialing and multiple telephone memories are available on most cellular telephones.

We recommend that if you apply for cellular service, use a reliable service provider (the larger the better, and generally a subsidiary of a wire service). This will ensure you can have the best area coverage possible.

Message Service

1. *Central Message Service.* There are many message services offered to those of us who travel extensively, and we have listed several in Appendix C. Your messages are taken and held for you for a specified time. You can then call to pick them up as stipulated between you and the message provider (usually within a specified holding time).

   You might check with your mail forwarding service to see if they also provide telephone message service. Also, check with your gasoline credit card provider, Good Sam, or

Discover Card. Some of them provide message service for a small fee—sometimes even free.

2. *Answering machine on your home telephone.* One benefit of having a stationary home (and telephone) is having a telephone answering machine that allows you to call and pick up messages, from anywhere, via a standard push-button telephone set. This method, however, requires long-distance calls monthly, also continual power service to your home, and a standard monthly phone bill.

3. *From Friends Or Relatives.* Although this method is probably the least expensive—because long-distance calls will be made only when necessary—it has its disadvantages. How often does your friend or relative move or change telephone numbers? Do you feel confident that they will take all your messages, or handle business calls correctly for you?

    As we decided with our mail needs, we felt it was better to deal with someone whose business it was to make sure we received the messages we needed. It has worked out well, and saves hard feelings.

4. *Computerized Voice Messaging Services.* There are as many of these services available as there are prices and ways that these services work. Basically, though, people can call and leave a voice-mail message for you. You then call and pick up those messages any time, usually with 24-hour service. With some, you can leave a message back to individuals—or you may want to return some calls personally. Look for services that provide a nationwide 800 number and a personalized voice mail box (see Appendix C for some available telephone message services).

. . . Staying Healthy?

We have found that many of the health problems we had when we were under the stress and strain of the everyday working world disappeared once we got on the road. As more time was available for adequate rest, proper diet, and exercise—and our general happiness with life itself increased—thus did our aches and pains disappear in equal measure.

Deanne had back problems (a herniated disc) that her doctor advised would require surgery. But she found that a month after being on the road, the backache that had plagued her for years disappeared. We think when stress leaves your lifestyle, you will experience the same freedom from stress-related illness we did.

"RV Knees" and some hints from "Townsend-oise"

One malady that has increased since we've crossed into middle-age is arthritis. One place we've noticed its presence is in our knees. We have asked many people if they tend to have pain on the insides of their knees (you know—the parts that knock together if you tend to be so inclined). Of the people we asked, those who were not full-timers said no. But of the ones who spend a great deal of time in their RV, there were many yeses.

Fancy or homemade entry steps can help prevent "RV Knees."

It took us awhile, but we finally determined that RV manufacturers generally use the same width (back to front) of entry
steps—which we use to get in and out of our home many times
a day. That width is smaller (and generally higher) than steps on
the front porches of houses.

Therefore (for us, anyway), we have to turn our foot sideways
and drop down onto the steps with all our weight as we leave the
RV. This daily regimen caused constant strain on our legs and
resulted in what we call "RV knees."

Gene solved this problem by building a platform that he
installs when we park, and breaks down and hauls in the truck
bed when we travel. This keeps our knees from any further
damage, but for the damage already done, we suggest two things
that may handle arthritis in your life.

Ocean Water. Remember Dr. Crane, who used to have a newspaper column from the '50s to the '70s? He recommended
drinking sea water in small quantities every day. He maintained
that this "magical medicine" contains forty-four trace minerals
that might help with such illnesses as Parkinson's disease and
arthritis. Dr. Crane said that arthritis is not something that is in
your body, but a lack of the right minerals in your system that
make your body healthy.

It works! When we lived in California, we went to the ocean,
filled a gallon jug of the stuff, and boiled it about twenty minutes
at a rolling boil. We then strained the sterilized water into a bottle
that would fit into the refrigerator, and each morning drank one
ounce. The pain disappeared.

If you don't live near the ocean, you can buy sea salt crystals
in health food stores, and dissolve them in plain water overnight.
Deanne's mother, who is now in her eighties, has drunk an ounce
of this water every day since 1974. Her hands were crippled and
painful before she began. The crippling has not gone away,
although it has not increased, but the pain is gone entirely. She
said if she stops this magical treatment for even three days, the
pain returns. So if you start, don't stop.

Don't drink more than an ounce a day. If you do, you may notice dry skin from the salt.

WD-40. If you're on a salt-free diet, perhaps you can try something else we've discovered: WD-40! Rub it on the painful places every night before you go to bed. Don't worry, it will quit smelling, and it isn't oily after it is rubbed in, so it won't get on the bedsheets.

It will take about two weeks of diligent application before you will notice the alleviation of pain—but it does work. Some pain, if severe, may take longer. Don't give up. Our WD-40 sits on the dresser so we don't forget. It may look ugly, but it's a great conversation piece when we take people on tours of our home.

You may laugh at these unique remedies, but as we've told many—they're cheap, they work, and if you don't like them, don't try them. It's your body.

. . . Banking, Credit and Debit Cards, Cashing Checks Out of State

Improvements in the banking industry, which have added worldwide branch office and use of automated teller machines (ATMs), have been a boon to full-timers. It used to be nearly impossible to cash out-of-state checks as we traveled. It has now become easy to obtain cash through ATMs, which use our bank's same access network (Versatel, IMPACT, CIRRUS, etc.).

Our bank issued us a handbook listing ATMs throughout the U.S. that use our network. We have rarely found that one of these ATMs was not within a reasonable driving distance. We hope, however, to see the day we will not only be able to withdraw money from our account, but also deposit money at different banks.

It remains true—and with the growth in security practices, more true all the time—that it is hard to cash out-of-state checks in grocery stores, banks not-our-own, and so on. We have taken several steps to avoid having to ask for this "special privilege":

- We keep a reasonable amount of cash with us, in our safe, for emergencies such as having no handy ATM when in need of groceries. The security (hopefully) of our permanently-mounted safe thus precludes the need for Traveler's Checks or Certified Checks, which we have often found hard to cash.

- We have bank accounts in Florida (our home state) and California (where we still do most of our business). Very handy.

- Use VISA and Mastercards to obtain cash from a teller's window at almost any bank. You might want to raise your credit limit before you leave "home," though.

- If you have a Money Market account, you can make good use of what is commonly called a "debit account." You put the money in, and they can issue you free checks—which are used just as you would use any other check. They may also give you a VISA card (which is called a debit card, though it is used just like a credit card). The beauty of a debit card is that there are no interest payments (since you are accessing your own money). You do not receive a bill—rather, a monthly statement, showing the activity in your account, and its balance.

Caution

> *You should be aware that money markets, although easily accessible, are not insured—and are thus not as safe as savings accounts. Don't put all your eggs in one basket.*

. . . Driver's Licenses

Most states require you to give up your driver's license from your previously lived-in state. You will want to check with your state-of-choice about their driver's license laws. Perhaps it won't matter if you don't keep your old license current. For us it was important, because we still bank in California.

You will have to go to your new home state and take the necessary tests to receive that state's license. You can then obtain driver's licenses by mail provided you don't get any moving violation tickets (in some states, and depending on your age).

. . . Licensing our Vehicle

Our home state of Florida requires that you physically have your vehicle in that state, where it can be inspected by an authority, when you register it for the first time. This gives them assurance that the identification number matches that which is on your registration slip.

This was our main consideration upon leaving California, because it was time to renew our registration. Thus, our first destination had to be our chosen home state. After the initial registration, though, it has been no different that it is for anyone else; we can continue to renew by mail. Some states will even allow you to register your vehicle for up to three years at a time.

. . . Insurance

RV Coverage

We have found very few insurance companies that offer full-timers the equivalent of a homeowner's policy, and recognize our right to live as we do. We use National General Insurance Co., and we found it available through Good Sam's VIP Insurance Program (you must be a member of the Good Sam Club). However, National General's insurance is also available through the Coast-to-Coast organization.

Others are Alexander & Alexander and Foremost Insurance Group, and although we cannot personally attest to their rates or benefits, we understand on good authority that they are reliable. In purchasing RV insurance, make sure you tell them you want *full-timer's* coverage, and that the agent understands your needs completely. You don't want to find out, in the heat of a claim, that you only have coverage that was sold to you as something that would "do the same thing."

Our motorhome is covered not only as a vehicle, but with visitor liability, as our home was covered with a homeowner's policy. Our point? Don't buy insurance assuming your agent is giving you what you need. S/he may only be hoping or assuming that's the case, and you may discover on the road that your insurance company isn't even aware of your special needs.

The Whale and the Guppy

As an example of people not understanding our lifestyle, a few summers ago we got into a situation that required Gene to drive into a field to turn the motorhome around and come back out through a gate. While making this big circle, he inadvertently drove through a sand pit and the rear tires immediately sank up to the hubs. By unhooking the truck, rocking the motorhome back and forth, and enlisting the help of local neighbors, we only succeeded in sinking deeper into the sand (and despair).

An hour or two later with much dirt inside, outside, and all over us, we drove our truck into town. We first called our insurance company—with whom we have emergency road service, who paid the cost with no problem. Next we phoned a tow truck. We carefully explained to the dispatcher that our mired vehicle was very large, and that he needed to send a very large tow truck. He felt sure he knew what we needed, and confidently sent a one-ton rig. However, the look on the driver's face when he saw the size of our "house" looking like a beached whale—and his rig a love-stricken guppy—almost made us laugh. If the situation hadn't been so frustrating, it would have been comical. We told him that we didn't think his tow truck could handle our problem, but he decided to try it anyway.

He hooked his winch to the front of our rig, parked one hundred feet away, and put it in gear; then yelled, "Heave!"—and the front of his truck went up like a rearing horse! He kept that winch pulling for all it was worth, which was just enough to allow the motorhome to drive itself out of its mired condition. We were completely out of the field in five minutes. I'll bet that man went home shaking his head with a story to tell that night. It was truly a sight.

Extended Warranties

You have probably read horror stories about extended warranties, and heard warnings against buying such warranties from the dealer who sells you your RV (rather than the manufacturer of your home on wheels). If you haven't been forewarned enough already, we hope that we can convince you, from our personal experience, to stay far away from such warranties:

We purchased our motorhome from a dealer in Southern California, and paid $1895 for an extended warranty. First, this insurance was virtually useless (every time we needed to use it, there was a reason why it was not valid). When we tried to cancel it and have a prorated amount returned to us, we found that our dealer was out of business. So were we. Eventually (only two years into this useless contract) we received a check for $166 from the original warranty company, who finally agreed to cancel our contract. We try not to think of what that $1895 is costing us in interest over the fifteen-year motorhome payment period.

If, then, you are not well advised to buy an extended warranty policy from the dealer, who should you buy one from? The manufacturer of your coach, themselves.

Life Insurance

Life insurance is a personal choice, and you will probably have such coverage when you begin to full-time anyway. Some service-providers who are part of a full-timers' life, such as Coast-to-Coast, Good Sam, and Family Motor Coach Association (FMCA) offer life insurance plans as well—plus a minimal amount of free Accidental Death & Dismemberment Insurance when you become a member of their organization. Consider: Anything offered free in this lifestyle will be worth looking into.

Health Insurance

Although those of you who are retired full-timers probably won't have this problem, the price of health insurance can be prohibitive when considering full-timing—especially for those with serious health problems. However, you might want to check the various supplemental insurance plans offered by such organizations as AARP, Good Sam, and Coast-to-Coast.

For those of us who are not of Social Security age, it is probably best to look into continuation of any health insurance policy you may have had in your stationary job. The rates should be somewhat reduced from buying an individual policy elsewhere.

Doctors

If you don't have the opportunity to purchase reduced-rate health insurance, you might consider one of the family health plans that are gaining in popularity throughout the U.S. The drawbacks to these plans might be:

• They may not provide nationwide coverage. Be sure and check.

• You may be sensitive about having a different doctor every time you need to see one. With traveling full-time anyway, you will probably run up against this problem with or without such a health plan.

Caution

> *Everyone—especially those with serious health problems—should carry their medical records (specifically those pertaining to their problem) with them in their RV.*

We strongly recommend having annual health checkups when you are in the area of your family doctor. This can help you avoid "emergency" checkups on the road, by someone who doesn't know you, or doesn't have your medical records.

5

WHAT ABOUT OUR
SPECIAL CIRCUMSTANCES?

"Are not two sparrows sold for a farthing?
And one of them shall not fall on the ground
without your Father. But the very hairs of your
head are all numbered. Fear ye not therefore,
ye are of more value than many sparrows."
Matthew 10:29-31

Loners (single, widowed, etc.)

We so admire those we've met on the road who travel alone. They are so full of life and willing to try anything. Their positive attitudes are sometimes awe-inspiring.

Years ago traveling alone would have been a situation that would have tried the stoutest of hearts. Especially those who would have been excluded from social activities.

But no more. The first and probably largest RV club for loners is Loners On Wheels (LoW), founded in 1969 by Edith Lane. This fast-paced and busy singles' group has fifty-two chapters throughout the U.S. They even have their own campground called "Lozark," near Popular Bluff, Missouri. These loners contend that being alone does not have to mean being lonesome. The club's size and number of activities ensure that those traveling alone need never be left out again.

Sometimes those looking for suitable companionship (in the RV world) advertise in the Classified Section of RV publications or newspapers. The many activities held at campgrounds are also an attraction for those seeking fellowship. So loners who do not wish to be alone need only open their eyes and look around.

Is Traveling *Alone* For You?

Gene feels that if something were to happen to Deanne, he would go on alone. He probably would buy a smaller rig, because he admits to deferring to Deanne when choosing what is necessity and what is luxury in a home.

Deanne, however, thinks she would find a place close to the kids again, and stop traveling. Don't hold her to it, though. We're sure there are many loners who felt the same way until faced with the prospect. Traveling grows on you, and once it becomes your lifestyle, staying in one place for very long can cause you to get itchy feet. We've already experienced a longing for the open road when only in a place for a few weeks. So, as Gene says to Deanne, "I'd like to see the day you stay in one place again."

Why would Deanne choose to put down roots if faced with the prospect of being alone someday? It's not because she can't drive the motorhome—or is afraid of being taken advantage of by ruffians. It's because there are so many things that can go wrong with a home that is put under the constant stress of movement. Her frustration with repairs that she knows nothing about (or finding someone to do it for her at a rate she probably could not afford) might build up fast.

Every time we have driven our home-on-wheels any appreciable distance, something has always gone wrong. Sometimes it may be a tiny thing, but just like it was when our home was stationary—it is and was always something. And our RV is probably no different from anyone else's.

For instance, during the writing of this chapter, while traveling from Michigan to California: 1. The bolts on the overload spring sheared and Gene had to physically remove the spring. This mild disaster forced Gene to crawl under the motorhome while on the freeway. 2. The pump motor wouldn't shut off. 3. There was a residue of transmission fluid leaking from God-knows-where under the motorhome's front end. 4. The horn button popped off when Gene pressed it to let someone who pulled out in front of us know he was about to cause our RV to merge permanently with his car. 5. Deanne broke off the rear-view mirror when Gene needed to check the frozen-up accelerator, and she had to change seats to drive (ah, the plains of Kansas in the wintertime). 6. The generator starter froze in the cold weather.

Then, to add insult to injury, when we pulled into the final stopping place, the S-10 had a flat tire. With a total of eighteen tires—on the motorhome, truck, and two bicycles—it seems that one of them is always flat. Don't let this example scare you though. This was an unusual trip; I guess we had just come into the law of averages for small problems this time.

Deanne hangs her head in shame at the number of lone women-travelers who are probably laughing, thinking she's faint-hearted. But it's something to consider: Are you knowledgeable enough to handle these typical situations that happen when your home is under the constant stress of moving? It's so important to know your own coach. We've saved so much money because Gene fixes anything that breaks, and detects something is wrong before it causes a disaster.

This is a very real consideration for lone travelers. As Deanne says, "Not every RV is built for living every day of your life in it. If we ever have one of those, and I'm alone at that point, ask me again—I sure want to change my mind!"

"Stuck" At Stuckey's

One of our more memorable trips was when Deanne had to spend several weeks on the west coast, while Gene and the motorhome remained in Florida. During that few weeks Gene had to move from one campground to another. This required a trip of fifty-five miles, and connecting and disconnecting the pickup by himself—four different times—once to go and once to come back—and twice on the way.

The worst part was that there was only one pair of eyes to do the job of two pair; there was no one to look ahead while traveling, to make sure Gene didn't get into a blind or tight spot while driving and towing the pickup. On this trip, in trying to locate a service station where he could obtain fuel, Gene wound up in spots where he had to disconnect the truck. Once he had to turn around, because he got off on a narrow road with no turnaround. Another time, at a Stuckey's service station, he had to back the rig (down a hill) to exit, as the service island had no pull-through.

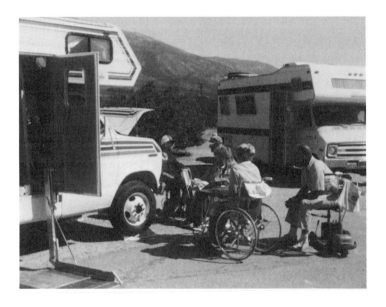

Disabled people enjoy life on the road.

Physically Challenged

Previously, if you were thought physically unable to travel, you probably never traveled. That thinking is outdated, because there are now many on the road who have met the challenge and have done something about it.

We have seen RVs equipped with wheelchair lifts, oversized doors, driving apparatus, and special handrails. Galleys that accommodate use of cabinets, tables, and appliances from a wheelchair, and many other concessions are now available and are shown in RV shows or advertised in brochures.

Active specialty RV clubs offer physically challenged individuals the opportunity to share fellowship, brainstorm common difficulties with solutions, and trade information about campgrounds and activities that service people with special needs.

One such club is the Handicapped Travel Club (HTC). They don't profess their main objective to be airing of their gripes—but to enjoy fun and fellowship. This should be the objective we all have for RV living.

6 ────────────────────────────────

WHAT ARE SOME RV SERVICES FOR FULL-TIMERS?

"They are all plain to him that understandeth,
and right to them that findeth knowledge."
Proverbs 8:9

Trip Routing

One benefit of joining such organizations as Good Sam Club, AAA, different gasoline company travel clubs, Coast-to-Coast, Family Motor Coach Association (FMCA), and clubs formed by manufacturers of RVs for their RVs' owners, is the ability to receive complete trip routing for all your trips.

Generally, you let the organization know where you are going, and they will help you plan your route. They ask pertinent questions such as your destination; whether you want to take the scenic route or travel major highways; and how much time you have to make the trip. Then they consult a detailed road map and give you information as to lodging along the way, road conditions, and other pertinent information.

We have found that full-timers can pretty well plan their own trips with a good Road Atlas and various handbooks listing large truck stops such as UNOCAL 76 and PETRO and campgrounds (public and private). But when you first "leave home," you might want to take advantage of trip routing for the experience. Later map out one on your own, just for the delight of knowing that planning is half the fun.

Campground Selection

It is this very subject that causes us to rejoice that we belong to private (membership) campgrounds. Before we had this convenience we were continually disappointed with campgrounds that had no vacancies without six months' prior reservations; camping sites that made us feel that we were parking in a supermarket's marked parking space (pavement and all); and dirty/full/destroyed/flooded restrooms and laundry facilities.

Parking on friends' property is a bonus to this lifestyle.

We can't say enough for our private campgrounds' access and availability. There is another approach that also has lent us praise: that of parking on friends'/relatives' property, and enjoying mutual friendships, family acquaintances, and solitude. We have some wonderful friends in Michigan, with beautiful property, where we can make necessary RV repairs at our leisure, and use tools that are too bulky to be carried with us on the road. This relationship allows us the privilege of working off any expenses for our being there (such as utility hookups and telephone) while we enjoy the camaraderie immensely.

Friendships made on the road thus prove to be mutually beneficial.

Reservations

Belonging to Coast-to-Coast is probably the best thing we did for ourselves before we left home. We can start out on a trek, confident that we can probably stay in any one of some five hundred resorts throughout the U.S. without calling ahead for reservations. Some campgrounds have a space-available policy, but in the whole time we've been on the road, we've only been turned away once. Sometimes we have had to park in what they call their boondock (or overflow) area, without hookups. However, we are always treated well and can enjoy the security and accommodations of the resort anyway.

We appreciate not having to make reservations because there are so many times when we're on the road and want to stop to see something. Thus, we want to spend a few extra hours—or even the night—which would cause us to arrive after our reservation grace period has lapsed. In not having to make such reservations, this stress is alleviated.

Thousand Trails requires a reservation and sometimes their more popular resorts are full during peak seasons. Again, we are treated well and can still enjoy the camaraderie from our boondock site. TAI, a relatively new, multiple-park, membership organization, has grown to over forty-eight parks, and has provided for its members a free 800 number for reservations.

Membership organizations listed under Trip Routing may also offer a travel service, which provides plane schedules, hotel and campground locations, ratings and rates, cruise, ski, and hotel discount packages, and road maps. As a result they can offer you the latest in what is available. This saves time, money, and frustration—not to mention telephone calls—in making use of the professionals who handle these services.

Facilities

Most campgrounds offer clubhouses, a pool, and other places and events to encourage us to socialize—the full-timer's way of networking. We so enjoy talking with people, especially those like us. We consider it a learning experience, because there is always someone anxious to share innovations in the RV world.

RV Clubs—Caravans

Sometimes, when we have nothing planned for a few weeks, we find ourselves wondering where to go next. We guess that comes from being busy for so many years, that to find ourselves without a goal makes us feel aimless.

It is at these times we get out all our RV magazines and start looking for a caravan or rally sponsored by one of our RV membership organizations. Once we even tried to plan a whole year ahead, to get to many of these "happenings"—even putting our event calendar on the computer! It didn't work out because we were soon off in another direction from the one we had planned, and found ourselves busy again. But one of these days we plan to get to more of these events.

Although full-timers are sometimes viewed as wanderers, there is no reason to feel lonely on the road. RV organizations familiar to all of us sponsor rallies, caravans to faraway places (either by driving your own rig in tandem, or loading it onto a train car—see Appendix A), visits to popular places such as Dollywood and San Simeon Castle, dinner/dances, football games, cooking contests, concerts, Tupperware parties, competitive sports events (such as chess games), and countless other activities. There is no reason for us to feel left out of society. We have our own.

Watch the magazines of the RV organizations to which you belong. They list a myriad of events where RV travellers gather. So many that you will be lucky if you can attend as many as interest you.

... And So On

RV financing, discount rates on gasoline and propane gas, emergency road service, credit card loss protection, travelers checks, VISA cards, monthly magazines, a legislative program, youth activities, emergency driver availability, classified advertising, membership directories, pet care and lost key service, and local service information through volunteer members are only a few of the other benefits available to full-timers. When you become a member of any RV organization, make use of all they offer your particular family. It will make your full-timing experience so abundant that you'll wonder how you ever had time to be a nine-to-five person.

7

OKAY, I'M CONVINCED; WHAT DO I DO?

"Every prudent man dealeth with knowledge:
but a fool layeth open his folly."
Proverbs 13:16

Reading About Full-Timing

Just when we think we know everything about this gypsy life, something new is introduced to full-timers. Then we get to add-to, pare-down, spruce-up, and buy a new gadget to make our life easier or more exciting.

In the last few years, there have been many books introduced into the market such as this one, and each offers different information than the last. While this book is not all-inclusive, we are happy you are reading it. We encourage you to obtain others to give you all the information you can get on this lifestyle. At your local library you will be surprised at the vast array of books, magazines, and newspapers to enlighten you.

RV magazines such as *Trailer Life, Motorhome, Woodall's, Highways*, and several RV monthly newspaper-type magazines proliferate, and occasionally offer specific information on full-timing. This is helpful, because the articles are written by many different RV'ers, with divergent requirements and viewpoints. As we have pointed out in the various chapters of this book, there are many approaches and answers to every challenge that we meet on the road. Therefore, having more than one opinion on any given subject can only ensure your ability to get a problem solved.

Talking to People Who Are Doing It

Before you make the final plunge into living in an RV, spend time at local campgrounds, RV stores, shows, and dealers. Talk to anyone who will listen and can give you pointers. Take it all in, filter it through your own like/dislike system, and use what fits to your own benefit.

We always enjoy going into other people's RVs and seeing what they have done to make their coach into a home. It may be foreign for you to ask, but a visit under a shadetree with someone who is working or just sitting outside their "home" nearly always turns into an invitation to "see how they did it." We try to make our home open to visitors in the same manner, and are eager to pick up hints and new ideas. If you have any to share, write us. You may then hear your suggestion touted in one of our seminars.

Planning It Your Way

In spite of all the material you will gather, and all the books you will read, in your own mind and heart you know what you want to do. These books are written to enhance that picture inside your heart, and give you knowledge to make it workable.

Renting Before Buying

We have met people on the road who feel that if they could begin again, they would choose another style of RV, think harder about a floorplan, keep some things they sold, and purchase items seen that they thought they would never need.

Life is a constant learning cycle, and we can't expect to know it all the day we hit the road. It may be of help for you to try living in an RV for a week's vacation without buying it. That way you will know at least what you *don't* want.

Recreational Vehicle Rental Association (RVRA) maintains a nationwide association of rental dealers. There are ads in newspapers, RV publications, and the local supermarket bulletin boards for RVs to rent. Somewhere among all these choices may be the style of RV that will become your next home.

We disagree on this point in RV living. Gene feels you can learn from an RV in a rented rig. Deanne argues that rented vehicles either have not been taken care of, are not set up properly, or have parts missing altogether. It seems to her that you might get discouraged unless you realize that when you get your own RV it will be different—and thus you can just enjoy the trip in your rented RV. We guess you need some type of familiarity with the life before you commit yourself and renting can be informative. We know of some (and are sure there are many others) who decided to full-time after spending some time in a rented RV. So pay your nickel and take your choice.

Section II:

Get Set!

8

WOW! WHAT CHOICES!

"But my God shall supply all your needs according
to his riches in glory by Christ Jesus."
Philippians 4:19

Generally, when most people—even those not new to RV life—think of full-timing, they think in terms of Gypsies. "Continually camping out" comes to their minds; in other words, "roughing-it," with hiking, backpacking, blisters, bugs, burned or undercooked food, and always—dirt. Ugh.

The truth is, we have everything in our RV that we had at home. Camping out full-time is not any more attractive to us than it is to the person envisioning such a thing.

Also, most people are surprised to discover the vast selection of choices available for our journeys:

A. **Motorhomes**: Class A; Van Conversions and Lo-Profiles (sometimes called Class B); and Mini's and Micro-Mini's (Class C).

B. **Trailers**: Travel Trailers, Weekend Warriors, Hi-Lo's, Fifth-Wheels, Park Models, and Tent Trailers.

C. **Pickup Campers**.

These veritable "wheeled palaces" come in every conceivable size (and price range), with an almost unlimited number of options and accessories.

Motorhomes

With entertainment centers containing TV's, VCR's, and fancy stereo players; comfortable reclining/swivel bucket seats; and a handy icebox (or refrigerator) for cold drinks while underway or at rest stops, you will quickly find that driving in your home is a wonderful way to travel! Especially traveling with children, as they can change seats and attend to bathroom chores without needing to stop. Of course, just as in commercial airplanes, they should return to their seats and refasten their seat belts as soon as possible.

Class A

This label classifies that broad category of rigs constructed on a truck or specially manufactured chassis—or even a converted bus. The Class A is easily recognizable because it is the same width from front to rear.

Class A motorhomes blend the driving area completely into the living area, and allow the "pilot" to drive the home while seated comfortably in his/her own living room. In many of these units, the driver and the passenger seats swivel around to become a part of the living room seating group. The husband of one couple we know tells us how his wife does just that, whenever they're traveling in the mountains. She said it helps not to have to watch the road and the vast expanse of horizon visible from the mountain roads, which causes vertigo for her.

Class A motorhomes are the units that come in the most extensive range of sizes (and, not surprisingly, with the broadest price spread). The Class A unit can be found in lengths ranging anywhere from 20 to 45 feet. They extend in price from a low of $29,000 to an astronomical $650,000. They vary from the small-family, one room, bunk house style, to the palatial bus with a queen-size bed in the bedroom, a glassed-in shower and jacuzzi-for-two in the bathroom, and a built-in bar—even equipped with an electronic bartender to mix drinks automatically for you.

Paradoxically, you will find that, generally, the smaller, less expensive units are designed for the family, that is for at least one adult and a few children. The large, plush, and expensive units, on the other hand, are designed for the retired couple, and have provisions for sleeping and seating only two people. There are exceptions in every size. We are quite confident that you can find yourself somewhere in one of these beauties.

One reason we wanted to buy a large Class A motorhome was that we could use a small vehicle towed behind the motorhome. This smaller auto would prove to be a gas-saver when unhooked and used for transportation during a stay at any one locality.

We also wanted a motorhome because we like the traveling as well as the stopping. It is much more comfortable to travel inside our home, with room to move about if necessary, and to work as we travel. Safety laws confine you to your seats, but Deanne finds it fun to sit at the desk, turn on the generator and computer, and write as we move.

It's much easier to pull into a rest stop, drop the jacks, and make lunch without going back into your unseen-for-two-hours home and finding what has fallen out of an improperly closed refrigerator. This often makes a bigger mess than would've been possible had you been able to turn around and see the door flying open. This is an experience we incurred with our first trailer. We were unable to rescue the carpet and had to have it replaced. What a mess! Thank goodness for checklists; see Chapter 16.

Finally, an uninhabited vehicle gets hot (or cold) while you travel. You have to take the time to open doors and windows, or turn on the heat before you can enjoy that eagerly-awaited meal or crawl into bed.

Normally the living area of a Class A motorhome is less than that of a fifth-wheel with the same length and floor space. However, we recently saw a new, 37-foot London Aire motorhome, made by Newmar Corporation, with a slide-out living room similar to those offered in a fifth-wheel. They offer a slide-out for the bedroom as well. The slide-out is now available on many different makes of motorhomes, including—among others—Space Craft and Allegro Bay.

The length of an RV is measured on the outside, from the rear bumper to the farthest point forward. Thus, often you will find that a 21-foot unit in one type of RV will provide more actual living area than a 26-foot unit in another type of RV.

Van Conversions and Lo-Profiles (Class B)

This RV, also sometimes known as a Class B unit, comes in lengths of seventeen to approximately twenty-one feet. We think the Van Conversion is probably the bait that frequently lures and traps people with the desire for and love of the RV life. Anyone who has ever traveled in one of these well-appointed "wheeled living rooms" has found it to be a most enjoyable way to get from Point A to Point B. We still remember fondly the cross-country trip we made with all three of our children, ages five, nine, and eleven at the time. We weren't even using a van conversion, merely a nine-passenger window van. We had outfitted it with sleeping bags in the rear where the kids could sleep, color, listen to music, or play quiet games as we traveled. They could move about as they became restless, and all of us arrived at our destination in great spirits.

Until recently, as the Lo-Profile RVs have been introduced, most of these units were designed only for riding comfort and waking livability. The sleeping and eating arrangements were not satisfactory. They are great and convenient travel units (some are even "garage-able"). Though the Lo-Profile RV comes with galley, beds and toilet facilities, we believe the Class B unit would be a hard stretch of endurance to qualify for use as a full-time living unit. We have met some very happy people, though, who live in this type of RV.

Once the newly-captured RV'er-to-be begins to look longingly at the "big ones"—the struggle to get free is over and RV fever is seemingly never overcome.

Mini-Motorhomes (Class C)

The broad designation of Class C is given to all rigs constructed on a "cut away" van (or pickup in the micro-mini) chassis.
The entire front of the vehicle, including dashboard, doors,
windshield, and engine cover—as well as the driver and passenger seats—is retained. It is like severing the vehicle right behind
the driver and passenger seats, leaving everything in the front
intact, and only the frame and drive-train in the rear. The
motorhome body is built onto the exposed rear frame.

These rigs are generally found from eighteen to twenty-nine
feet in length. A few of the longer units may even have tag axles
installed behind the drive wheels. They are, as a rule, easy to
recognize due to the "cab-over" area being built over the top of
the front driving area.

One pitfall you may run into (especially in an older used
vehicle) is that with the addition of dual wheels on the rear, many
builders used incompatible wheel sizes front to rear. This is not
a real problem for a weekend vehicle, but if you have to carry
spare tires for the rear and the front of your motorhome—as well
as for your towed vehicle—space and weight may become a real
problem. Then try to remember which size is used where, which
ones were last changed or rotated, or figure out how to rotate
them, and locate a dealer with the proper sizes when necessary.

The Class C motorhomes also come in a vast array of price
and options. The typical new price for the current models runs
from $21,000 to close to $120,000 for the more luxuriously
appointed units. Virtually all of the options found on Class A
units are also available for Class C units.

Micro-Mini's

These units are built on the mini-truck chassis (the light utility
pickup such as a Datsun, Toyota, or S-10). In former years the
safety of these units was questionable, due to the overloading of
the original truck chassis. Many of the first manufacturers of
these units were not scrupulous regarding gross vehicular weight

limitations of the chassis, also of the factory equipped tires and wheels. Therefore, we stress caution to anyone who considers purchasing a used unit if it is older than a 1990 model. In recent years however, the Federal Highway Safety Commission has established safety requirements and follow-up checks to prevent this problem.

You'll find these rigs wherever you find full-timers, and those who use them are generally quite satisfied with their handling and performance. However, apparently their living and storage space is limited, and full-timing in such cramped quarters might prove stressful.

All of the standard features found on a typical Class C motorhome may be found on the micro-mini.

Trailers

The word "trailer" is the broad title used for any type of towed conveyance, whether used for living in, or for carrying another vehicle (such as a car or a motorcycle). However, for our discussion here we will only consider those trailers that will be lived in.

In these days when the EPA has firm control over the numbers and types of engines produced by automobile manufacturers, very few people are using cars for tow vehicles and are forced to use pickups or vans. So the largest drawback to full-timing in a trailer is that the tow vehicle often becomes the runabout transportation. It generally has minimal seating capacity and low fuel mileage (as with using a pickup truck for the tow vehicle).

Also, we met some people on the road who did not feel as safe in their trailer as they might have in a motorhome or other totally-contained rig. Some surly-looking characters had knocked on their door in a rest stop late one night. They felt that if they had owned a motorhome, they could simply have started the engine and driven away. In the trailer rig they needed to go outside and around, to get into their truck to leave.

On the positive side, although a trailer isn't as much fun for traveling, its living space probably makes it the most comfortable type of RV to live in once you're stopped and "set up."

Travel Trailers

For those not familiar with the RV world, a trailer brings visions of the non-self-contained travel trailer of the past. This unit has come a long way since the Lucille Ball/Desi Arnaz movie, *The Long, Long Trailer*. They have become much lighter with the use of modern space age materials instead of the hardwood framing and plywood interiors of that era. Perhaps with a modern lightweight unit, Lucy could have taken her rocks without so many mishaps!

The units of today are also more self-contained with their powerful generator sets, efficient power converters, and large capacity water and holding tank systems. They come equipped with more amenities than even Lucy could have made a mess of.

The travel trailer is the basic full-timing rig, the one that almost all of the "purists" used initially. Some, even today, don't consider that you are a real RV'er unless you use the travel trailer. However, our purpose here is to reveal the advantages and disadvantages of each type of unit without prejudices.

Because a travel trailer now is pretty much what a house trailer used to be in size and comfort, it seems to look the most at home when parked in a campground. Deanne believes if people thought they couldn't be happy living in an RV, they should imagine their house or apartment squeezed down in space, but still given the same amenities (with drapes, separate rooms, and all). Then they'll know what it is to live in a travel trailer.

The travel trailer generally comes with all the features and accessories that can make this type of rig a home. They range in lengths of fourteen to thirty-seven feet, with prices ranging widely from $8,000 to well over $90,000 for the top-of-the-line units.

The Weekend Warrior

The Weekend Warrior is an innovation in the travel trailer stable. It is a fully equipped, self-contained travel trailer, which can be converted into a garage for dune buggies and motorcycles. A small galley and bath are located in the front-end of this unit; the gaucho beds and dinette fold against the side walls to provide the "parking area" in the back. A factory option with this arrangement is a ramp built into the back wall, which is used to load the vehicle(s) into the trailer.

The Weekend Warrior may also be considered for use as a garage for a small towed vehicle, as discussed in Chapter 10.

Hi-Lo's

This special type of travel trailer is manufactured by the Hi-Lo Corporation. It collapses to about half its normal height while being transported. These units are available in a limited range of sizes and come with fewer amenities than do standard trailers; however that range is also surprising.

Few full-timers consider this unit to be adequate. However, we have seen them in use by those who find that by using a Hi-Lo and a given tow vehicle they can get a bit more distance out of their fuel dollar. Any unit is more acceptable than not to full-time at all. Hi-Lo Corporation came out with its own version of the fifth-wheel in 1989. However, the local dealer told us that the model did not catch on well, and was only manufactured that one year.

Fifth-Wheels

The fifth-wheel is a unique innovation and has been quite prevalent over the last twenty-five to thirty years of RV travel. Based on the design of the large tractor-trailer trucks, there are several reasons for this trailer's great popularity:

- The length of the unit is also the total usable living space; for example, if the unit is twenty-six feet long, there is also twenty-six feet of usable living area. In the standard trailer, a twenty-six-foot unit will have approximately five feet of its length used by the tongue, which cannot be included in the living space computation. To have the same twenty-six feet of living area, the trailer would have to be thirty-one feet long. Slide-outs can also add many square feet to the living areas of the galley, dinette, living room, and bedroom. These are available in both trailers and fifth-wheels.

- The hitch is under the front raised portion of the unit and rides over the bed of the tow vehicle (normally a standard pickup truck) above its rear axle. This shape makes the complete length for any given fifth-wheel with its tow vehicle approximately ten to twelve feet shorter than it would be for the same length standard trailer and its tow vehicle.

- The fifth-wheel also has a much reduced turning radius because the trailer begins its turn at the location of the rear wheels of the tow vehicle. Because of this shape, the tow vehicle can also turn at a very sharp angle (greater than ninety degrees). This allows the driver to be able to back the fifth-wheel into much tighter spots than possible with a standard trailer of the same length.

The fifth-wheel is one of the most popular choices for the full-time life. It allows maximum usable floor space—especially with its slide-out living room, galley, and/or bedroom areas—and offers many exciting and different floorplans.

It comes in as many different choices and prices as can be imagined. Typical prices range from $14,000 to over $100,000 for a unit with luxurious amenities.

Park Models

These are not self-contained travel-trailers, but are designed for use only in full hookup parks. Many "snowbird" parks will only allow this type of trailer on their grounds. They are not normally towed around by full-timers in their trailers, but are generally located in either their home base or in a destination park to be used as a winter or summer home. In former years these units were called "trailer houses."

Park models are normally delivered and set up in much the same manner as the modern mobile or modular home. Most of them are towed into place and the running gear (tongue, axles, and wheels) removed. They are then set on blocks with permanent plumbing, electrical, and telephone services hooked up.

These units also have a wide price range and their sizes vary considerably. Some of them have full-size tilt-outs, versus the slide-outs found on their "traveling cousins," and others may come with carports and screened porches or patios. The list goes on and on; it would be impractical to describe them all in this type of book. Park models are not the type of RV that travelers can take with them, the whole premise for this book. The best way to learn about park models is to ask for brochures from a local distributor.

Tent Trailers

The modern hardtop tent trailer is the ultimate in tenting. It allows the tent to have a permanent floor raised off the ground with a solid roof over the main area. Some of them even have a built-in water system with sink and toilet facilities, a cooktop, an icebox or refrigerator, and permanent beds.

We are convinced that, even with these appointments, the tent trailer is marginal for being of practical use as a full-time home. The problem of heating it efficiently is only one of its several drawbacks. Personal security also ranks high on the list of disadvantages. However, we have met some on the road who are quite happy with this unit.

Pickup Campers

These versatile and seemingly ageless units are found in almost every campground, park and driveway throughout the U.S. We believe the pickup camper is the flagship for the groundswell of modern nomads who have taken to the American highways in the last four decades. This type of unit, more than any other, has sparked the romance between traveling in the beloved automobile, and the ability to take your home on the road.

The pickup camper is another of the RV units with such a vast array of styles that the uninitiated RV traveler tends to confuse it with the motorhome. In actuality, the category "pickup camper" encompasses a range of units from the simple "bed topper" all the way to the twelve-foot units with a king-sized, cab-over bed, designed to sleep up to six adults (there may be some longer units, but they would be rare).

Many of these units have "pass-throughs" or "crawl-throughs" installed in place of the rear window of the pickup truck. This allows the feeling of the camper section and the truck cab being one unit. These crawl-throughs also tend to make the camper more permanently attached to the pickup body. Thus enters the confusion between the camper and a motorhome.

The pickup camper is designed to be mounted within the bed (most of it, anyway) of a standard production pickup truck that has the proper weight-carrying specifications. Once it is mounted, though, many owners tend never to remove it because it is not easy to do (especially with the crawl-through). Besides, it just seems more convenient to leave it where it is. In some states, the way it is licensed determines whether it is legal to remove the camper or not. It is sold as a separate unit and is still considered separate from the truck that carries it. Some states even require a separate license.

The pickup camper is pressed into service as a full-time home by vast numbers of people. Many of them are full-timers who love to travel the great wilderness areas of this country. The four-wheel-drive pickup with a camper on the back can go almost anywhere a road or jeep trail has been cut. This is the reason for the wide range of sizes and styles available. The venerable old pickup camper has established many a hunter's camp.

Class A Motorhomes have the same width, from front to rear.

Class A motorhomes allow the drivers to pilot their homes while seated comfortably in their living rooms.

*Now **this** home is classy.*

Newman's double slide-out motorhome.

Expanded living room via slide-out in motorhome.

A 13-foot slide-out is also available.

Van conversions—the bait to hook RV'ers.

Class C motorhomes are recognizable by their cab-over area.

A Micro-Mini is built on a light utility pickup frame.

This travel trailer is the basic full-timing rig.

Hi-Lo trailers can save fuel dollars.

The Hi-Lo fifth wheel.

The fifth wheel is one of the most popular choices for RV life.

*Security risk ranks high on the list of
disadvantages of the tent trailer.*

Fancy tow rigs allow whole families to ride together.

A pickup camper awaiting its pickup.

9

LET'S FIND OUR DREAM HOME

*"For a dream cometh through the multitude of business;
and a fool's voice is known by a multitude of words."*
Ecclesiastes 5:3

When we first began looking for our full-time home, we were stunned (and confused) by the total market. We found that there were too many choices for us to make a rational decision concerning any RV-home without having a plan.

Thus, we began by seeking help to determine what to look for. We turned to RV magazines and other books of this type, and sought the advice of those we met who were already full-timers. These step-by-step goals and advice, which we pass on to you with our own suggestions in turn, are:

1. Determine your basic needs.

2. Determine your own tastes (or desires) in an RV.

3. Determine your financial capability (realistically).

4. Rent or otherwise experiment to decide what you can live with (see Chapter 7).

5. Don't wait too long or you'll never do it (See Chapter 1).

Goal No. 1: Determining Our Basic Needs

We broke this first goal into two, easier-to-take, one-at-a-time steps:

First Step: Size of Unit

We had to decide what size unit we wanted. We planned to live only in our unit, with no home base, so we had to have a rig that was big enough to hold all our belongings. This eliminated the pickup campers, tents, and so on. It also put us in the category of the higher-priced models, which were built stronger and had more and better storage features.

Next Step: Type of Unit

The next step was to decide between a trailer (fifth-wheel or standard travel trailer) and a motorhome (probably Class A, because of the size limitations).

Since we planned to spend a great deal of time traveling, we decided it would be handier for us to work while we drove if we had access to the portable computer, reference material, and office tools. We could have the luxury of fixing a sandwich while we traveled—and could enjoy the scenery from our own living room.

Thus we decided that the Class A motorhome was our rig of choice. If we had planned to spend more time parked than traveling, we probably would have opted for a fifth-wheel. It could, according to many people, provide a more home-like interior, but probably would not be as much fun while we were on the road.

Many people are dismayed by the high cost of replacing a motorhome when it wears out, versus the cost of replacing a worn-out tow vehicle. While this cost is significant, we chose another approach to the problem. We made our motorhome into the home of our choice—with modifications, additions, and so on. Now we merely have to repair or replace the engine or drive train at a considerably lower cost than that of replacing a tow vehicle.

Goal No. 2: Determining Our Own Tastes/ Desires for Our Home

The following list may not contain some items you need, or even want, to live comfortably in your RV home. We offer it to you as a guide to get you started.

As we shopped, we kept this list with us. If not in hand, it was in our minds, because we had taken the time to compile it. In this manner, it was easier not to become confused. We had narrowed our choice to a motorhome, and a Class A was the only size that would fit a desk and island bed. We thus eliminated needlessly looking at the other types of RVs.

The Minimum Guidelines While Searching for Our Full-time Home

1. Queen-size island bed
2. Dinette in the galley
3. Separate living room area
4. Large tub and/or shower
5. Adequate closet space
6. Plumbing/heating ducts clear of storage space
7. Outlets in logical places
8. Side or rear bath (not split)
9. Generator
10. Microwave oven
11. Four-burner stove/oven
12. Quality carpeting
13. Air conditioner(s)
14. Exit doors on both driver and passenger sides
15. Room to add a roll-top desk
16. Lots of outside storage (see basement models)
17. Large refrigerator with separate freezer
18. Adequate galley storage
19. Enough bedroom drawers
20. Use of all the available bedroom wall space
21. LP gas detector
22. Smoke alarm
23. TV antenna
24. Large holding tanks
25. Electronic ignition modules for furnace, refrigerator, water heater

Goal No. 3: Determining Our Financial Capabilities

Our third goal flowed naturally behind Goals One and Two—deciding our basic needs versus tastes and desires.

Our finances were no different from anyone else's, so we realized that having everything on our list would price it out of our range.

While we agreed there were wants we could do without, there were others that were important. As we compared the list to the RVs, we realized there were also some options that couldn't be changed once we bought the coach (for example, a table in the galley area, or a separate living room area). Yet there would be other things we could do without until adding them ourselves, to afford our coach. We always looked to see if there was room to make these improvements. Then we would discuss what we were willing to accept as tradeoffs.

The dinette serves a multitude of purposes.

As it happened, we shopped for several years before we found the exact coach for us. By that time, with all our experience, we knew our rig when we walked into it.

If we had only one piece of advice to give you when shopping for your RV, it would be to avoid impulse buying (whether at RV shows, personal sales, or on an RV lot). After all, this is to be your home. Take the same care in buying it as you would in purchasing any house.

Take the time to make your list, so that you don't get wrapped up in the decor, and find (too late) that it never dawned on you to see if there was adequate closet space or drawers. One of Deanne's pet peeves is storing canned goods above the bed, or sheets in the galley or living room cabinets.

What Can We Expect?

Determination of Features

Every type and style of modern RV has its own special features, but following is a list of those that are standard on most of the RVs today, with a few of the many standard options:

Galley and dining. All units worthy of consideration for the full-timer should have a complete galley. This includes at least a cooktop, refrigerator, sink, and dining area large enough for all of the family to sit and eat together. We have some friends who thought a dinette table was not important, as there were only two of them. They reasoned that they could easily fit at the little table provided in the living room area. This, however, soon became an important irritant. They had to carry food back and forth from the "kitchen," and the wife tripped over her husband and disturbed his ball-game watching every time she set the table. When the meal was ready, this tiny table wasn't big enough to hold both the place settings and the food. They had to set the serving dishes on the couch or eat buffet-style and each go fill their plate at the stove. They finally traded for a two-foot longer unit with a dinette table at a considerable loss in the transaction.

We simply can't live without a table, because, just as in a conventional home, so much more is done on it than just eating. And it holds a multitude of odds and ends!

Following is a list of the available equipment and options to be found on the modern RV galley:

1.   *Refrigerator/Freezer (Optional).* Few late model RVs come equipped with the older icebox units; however, very inexpensive travel trailers, pickup campers, and van conversions may still be so equipped. We don't consider an icebox to be at all suitable for the full-timer. The supply of ice is limited to retail stores and/or campgrounds with full services. Usually the ice doesn't last very long, especially in the summer, when it is most needed. Also, an icebox is not cold enough to properly maintain food for any length of time.

     The refrigerator/freezer found on almost all self-contained RVs is of the absorption type. Park models usually come equipped with small, apartment-sized, standard refrigerators. The absorption units have no moving parts, and when properly leveled tend to require no maintenance except the occasional defrosting.

2.   *Ice Maker (Optional).* The ice maker option is one that most people will find hard to justify; however, on hot, dusty summer days, that never-ending supply of cubes for those tall glasses of lemonade is justification enough. Practically speaking, though, this feature is convenient, but optional. They are good only if you spend most of your time in a full-hook-up park somewhere, because they require AC power and a constant flow of water.

3.   *Cooktop Range (Oven Optional).* A range and oven sounds like a simple constant, but in today's modern marketing scheme you should be aware that many RV

manufacturers don't include the oven, but supply only a cooktop. They have decided that a "browning" or "convection" type microwave oven can replace the old-fashioned baking oven. Deanne admits to being an indifferent cook, so if she needs an oven, probably so do most people. If baking is important to you, beware!

4. *Vent Hood/Light.* All late model RVs are equipped with some form of vent hood for the cooktop. This will help to eliminate odors when you cook, and removes any smoke from frying or toasting. It can also help prevent your smoke detector from sounding off unexpectedly.

5. *Microwave Oven (Optional).* A microwave oven may not be an option if you run into a unit mentioned in Number Three above. We find we don't know how to cook without one anymore.

6. *Galley Sink.* The size of the galley sink for the full-timer is something to consider. The main reason for this is that the ordinary "camper" size sink is too small and shallow to put a standard size dinner plate in the water. So be sure to look for a unit with a sink size suitable for your needs.

7. *Water Heater (With Optional Electric Heating Element).* What can be said about a water heater? If you don't like having to get up in the morning and traipse outside in the wind or rain to relight it to take a shower, look for a unit with an electronic ignition module.

You also may be interested in a water heater with an optional electric heating element, but beware! Some campgrounds charge extra for this convenience. The reason for this option is that it maintains constant hot water (without the worry of running out of LP gas) and is silent in its operation.

8. *Water Filter (Optional).* A water filter may be a necessity if you're sensitive to the various and sundry microbes in

the water systems of different places, especially south of the border.

9.   *Food Storage.* Every RV unit has varying numbers of cabinets, pantry, and storage places for groceries, cooking utensils, flatware, and dishes. Only you can decide if a particular unit will meet your needs, according to the way you cook, buy groceries, and generally stock your larder.

A word of caution: Check the insides of cabinets. Sometimes what looks like a large cabinet is reduced in space/utility by pipes or heater vents.

10.   *Dining Area or Dinette/Foldout Table (Optional).* The size of your family and how you plan to entertain will determine how much dining space your home requires. Re-read the introduction to Galley and Dining if you are considering eliminating this feature. You can't easily add a table later without buying a new coach.

Living Areas. To live full-time in an RV unit, we feel strongly that careful consideration should be given to the area that will provide your daytime living activities. Often you will find that inclement weather, travel, illness, or some other factor will prevent you from "living" on the outside of your unit. It's at these times you will prove the suitability of your rig to your family's needs.

We believe that definite consideration of the following will help you in deciding what constitutes your RV home:

1. *Seating.* There must be adequate and comfortable seating (gaucho, swivel chairs, and outdoor seating) for each member of your family. Everyone should, at some time, have a place they can call their own.

2. *Entertainment Devices.* TV, radio, and other entertainment devices should be considered as important to you in your full-time RV home as they were to you in your previous home.

A TV will keep you informed about what the rest of the world is enduring, and help you plan your travels with relatively accurate weather reports. CD's and tape players will allow you to relax with your favorite sounds, wherever you may be. Many people also use CB, ham, SWL, and computers as entertainment while on the road. Your own abilities with guitar, harmonica, keyboard, or other musical instruments, can also be accommodated. We've even met people with small spinet pianos and organs in their units.

3. *Room Lighting.* Lighting is something that may not even enter your minds; however, over time the type of lighting provided will enhance the feeling of "home." We have found that more or brighter lights are not the answer; most important is the type of lighting. Because of space limitations, we purchased a pair of wall-mounted swing arm lamps, which provide the necessary shaded, incandescent lighting to make our living room feel like home.

4. *Carpeting.* Most of the new RVs (except the rock-bottom priced units) come equipped with carpeting. Many new and very expensive units now come with parquet floors in the galley and ceramic tile in the bath area. However, we have found throw rugs and small area rugs personalize the rig and protect the original carpeting from spills and everyday grime. Look for tips on how to anchor these throw rugs to keep them where you want them and prevent tripping in Chapter 14.

5. *Decorative Items.* Pictures and decorator items are as varied as the individuals who need them to feel at home. In Chapter 14, we include tips on how to fasten these items to walls, shelves, and cabinets without risk of damage to the items or the rig.

6. *Heating.* Modern RVs come equipped with an LP (liquefied propane) gas-fired furnace. There are four types of heating units in use in the industry:

A. *Radiant Heater*. These may be obsolete, but many are in use. The radiant heater (no fans or other moving parts) is usually found in the less expensive or older trailers and motorhomes. This was the type we had in our first seventeen-foot trailer, and it was quite adequate.

B. *Forced Air Furnace*. This 12-volt, forced-air-fan furnace is currently the standard. It is a small version of the type used in homes throughout the U.S. This furnace is controlled by a wall-mounted thermostat. In larger units, one of these thermostats may be found in the front of the coach, and one in the rear, each controlling a separate furnace.

C. *Catalytic Heater (Optional)*. The last type of LP gas heater is the catalytic heater—a very efficient unit that does not have any moving parts or flames.

Warning

> *Catalytic heaters come in many styles and types. Some of them are not vented to the outside of the coach, nor do they have provisions for drawing fresh air from the outside for combustion. Please be advised—when using an unvented type, you must open a roof vent or window to allow fresh air into the RV.*

D. *Electric Space Heater (Optional)*. An alternative to the LP gas furnace is one of the many ordinary electric space heaters available. Many full-timers have discovered how efficiently one of these tiny units can heat the relatively small area of an RV. Generally, these heaters require that you park in a full hookup park, and you may need to pay for the electricity used.

7. *Cooling (Optional)*. Most full-timers will not consider this an option. However, in the purchase of a new RV the air conditioner is not a normal standard equipment item. There are other types of cooling devices that must be mentioned here—some that work quite well in some parts of the country and not so well in others. Also, because there are other types of cooling equipment available the dealer cannot presume to know your choice or even where you plan to travel. The three basic cooling devices are:

A. *Air Conditioner (Optional)*. This is the refrigeration type with a compressor/condenser closed system. These units are rated in BTU's (British Thermal Units) and have several advantages:

- A refrigeration type unit has the greatest ability to provide a cool environment because it can create the greatest differential from the inside to outside temperature.

- These are thermostatically controlled and, under most circumstances, can maintain the desired level of comfort.

- These units are designed as one-piece units that require only that power (120 vac) be at the location on the roof where they are installed. Most RV manufacturers have pre-wired their RVs to be "air conditioner ready."

- These units are unobtrusive to the interior of the RV and some newer models are even flush to the ceiling and unnoticeable.

There are a few disadvantages:

- The most obvious disadvantage is the requirement for shore-power (or the operation of the generator and its attendant noise) to operate it.

- Another disadvantage is the greater amount of interior noise inherent in the operation of these units.

- In dryer areas, these units can cause dry skin and irritate the sinuses, among other maladies.

B. *Evaporative Coolers (Optional)*. These are also known as "swamp-coolers" and are prevalent in use in the south, southwest, and the more arid sections of the country. Some advantages for this unit are:

- The initial cost for this type of cooling unit is quite low.

- The operational cost is low.

- This type of unit is available for the RV that operates on 12 vdc.

Some disadvantages are:

- They are only effective where the ambient humidity is quite low (below 25%).

- They will raise the humidity within the home or RV as they operate.

- Besides requiring power (120 vac or 12 vdc) to the roof opening, these units also require a source of water for the evaporator pads.

- The cooling efficiency is not as great as with the air conditioner, but for the difference in cost (and if we remember the limited areas of effectiveness), we believe this unit has promise.

C. *Fans (Optional)*. Many manufacturers will include a fan or two in their design. However, usually additional fans for moving the air must be added by the user. A fan merely gives the *effect* of cooling. It does not lower the ambient temperature in the room where it is operating, except by moving cooler air from some other source into the room; for instance from a room that has air conditioning into a room without it.

There are numerous fans available to fit a small RV space.

Fans help us to feel cooler by passing air over our skin, causing the moisture to evaporate from it, and thus lowering our skin surface temperature. There are many types of fans available, and most of them are either designed for use in an RV or can be adapted for RV usage. There are 120 vac fans and 12 vdc fans available.

There are tabletop fans, floor fans, window fans, roof-vent fans, ventilator fans, ceiling fans, defroster fans and (if you will recall those warm Sunday mornings, the "Church Bulletin" fan) even hand-held fans.

Sleeping Areas

1. *Permanent Beds.* A bedroom (or at least the cabover area) holds the secret to being at home while living in your RV. Some nights you may just not feel like, or even be able to, convert the dinette or the gaucho into a bed. These will be the times when you will even question why you are out there.

You will just want to crawl into a comfortable bed and pull the covers up over your head (without being in the middle of someone else's dinner).

A separate bedroom is important for those days when one of you is ill and needs to be away from the rest of the family. Most important, not everyone likes to get up at the same time. It can be a real irritant if you want to sleep in, while someone else wants to make breakfast—on your bed!

Finally, making the bed is important if it's in the middle of your living room, while if it is in a separate room, you can just shut the door.

2. *Conversion Beds.* Gauchos, dinettes and fold-down bunks are, for the most part, designed for the grandchildren or the over-nighter, not for the full-timer. While many people are full-timing in this manner, we know that they would enjoy it more if they had a permanent bed with a good mattress.

   Children are generally comfortable in a cab-over bed, but if they're small, they may fall out. We have seen an innovative use for those tailgate nets used on the back of pickup trucks. They fit nicely across the front of a cab-over bed, making a soft guardrail. Because they're flexible, they also fold up conveniently if the cab-over bed pushes up to the ceiling when not in use.

3. *Sleeping Rooms (Optional).* This is an option available to those rigs that are equipped with awnings. They are little more than tents that use the RV side as one wall and the awning as the roof. We can't imagine using this for a permanent bedroom, especially in the winter or rainy season, considering how waterproof most awnings are (or aren't)!

Bath Facilities

If there was any one feature that could have prevented our entrance into the world of full-timing, this was it. Gene can still remember a tent camping trip into a National Forest with all of the kids. We planned to spend one week camping out and hiking through the forest trails, enjoying nature, and being free. Thirty-six hours later, we were driving all over the mountainside trying to locate a shower for Deanne.

Thus, our rig had to have specific appointments pertaining to the bathroom: A) Gene required that the shower have enough headroom for him to stand upright. B) There was to be a tub and shower combined. C) The tub/shower was to be in the bathroom (no split bath for us because we didn't want to step out of the shower into the hallway). D) We had to have adequate storage for toiletries in the bathroom itself.

Consider the following when listing requirements for your RV bathroom:

1. *One-Piece Unit.* A toilet unit where the shower, toilet, and sink (lavatory) are all in the same tiny area (all within the shower). A shower curtain protects the doorway and toilet paper from the shower spray.

   These units are found in many very short rigs and in some smaller Class C motorhomes. We believe that these units are designed for camping only, and are inadequate for two people to use full time. After one has showered, the entire bathroom—toilet, sink, walls, and ceiling—may continue to drip for an hour or more and will be highly uncomfortable to use. This will require that any teeth-brushing or shaving will have to take place elsewhere—either in the galley, the public restrooms, or outside.

2. *Split-Bath Units.* Split baths have the tub/shower unit on one side of the RV and the toilet/lavatory on the other side. This is quite a common arrangement in many motorhomes and in several fifth-wheels. Occasionally you may see it in conventional trailers.

   The biggest objection we have to this arrangement is the requirement that the entire rear of the coach be shut off from the front while someone is in the shower. Otherwise, someone will either get a surprise or give everyone a show when they step out into the hallway.

3. *Tub/Shower Combination.* Tub/shower combinations are similar to the ever-popular arrangement found in the American home. In this instance the tub is generally downsized and custom designed to fit into the space available in the RV. Most of these units come with an installed shower curtain and a hand-held showerhead with a shut-off to conserve water. This is the minimum requirement, we think, for adequate bathing facilities.

Deanne says she really likes those beautiful shower-only arrangements she has seen in the expensive coaches. However, the tub is useful for washing items too large for the sink (like the venetian blinds).

The location of the bathroom is somewhat important to most people, and very important to others. If you are sensitive about people walking through your bedroom, a rear bath model of motorhome would be a poor choice for you. These rigs generally have a pair of twin beds on either side of the aisle leading to the rear bath. However, the split bath is common in both the fifth-wheel and the Class A motorhome. It allows visitors to use the vanity and commode without having to enter the bathing area. As you can see, it is wise to consider many factors when making these decisions.

Storage

To the full-timer, this is one subject that must be considered from the beginning. In Chapter 2, we talked about how to reduce your possessions and keep only those that are required. Once you've reached your goal, you must find a place for everything you've decided to keep.

In our home, if one of us finds a six-inch space that isn't being used for anything, we're as excited as if we had bought a new china cabinet! It becomes assigned as "a place" immediately, because space is so limited. We quickly learned that space is a valuable thing to waste; don't fill it unnecessarily.

A corollary to this is also a byword to the successful full-timer, "A place for everything, and everything in its place." This is a necessary rule in tight quarters. Not only will things get lost or stepped on, but it will quickly become an irritant of major proportion when your only seating area is covered with things that should be put away.

1. *Conventional Versus Basement Models*. Conventional RVs differ from basement models in their construction. The conventional RV usually has its outside storage areas carved from concealed areas or compartments inside the rig. This is the type of unit that we are currently using, but the day we trade up, we'll definitely get a basement model. At the time we purchased our rig there were no basement models available. In fact, Gene mentioned a plan for a basement model to one RV manufacturer, and the next year it appeared on the market. He wonders if he missed his calling as an RV designer.

   The basement model is built with a double floor frame (tending to raise the living area higher off the ground). This allows room for all tanks, plumbing, and storage areas, under the floor, in the "basement." Not only does this provide more storage, it lowers the center of gravity if all of your heavier items are stowed beneath the floor.

   The floor in these units is raised above the vehicle frame, allowing for the provision of full-width compartments. This permits the storage of long and bulkier items such as skis, umbrellas, and flagpoles. Another important advantage to the basement model is the ability to prevent freezing of holding tanks and water lines. Most manufacturers run the heat ducts in the basement area.

2. *Inside Storage*. Inside compartments and cabinets are generally used for food, day-to-day living items, everyday clothes, and shoes.

Basement models provide full-width, pass through compartments.

3. *Add-on Pods.* Pods are an easy way to extend your storage space, but will tend to raise your center of gravity and increase the wind resistance. In our case, we installed a pod to carry our seasonal clothing and luggage (sometimes our work calls for us to travel separately; thus luggage is required).

What If Money Is No Object?

Plan For A New Dream

1. 36' to 40' length slide-outs
2. Diesel pusher (hopefully a bus conversion)
3. Queen-size island bed
4. Parquet floor in galley
5. Built-in fireproof safe
6. "Home" size/depth sinks
7. Ice maker
8. Rear-view TV camera system
9. Power seats
10. Air horns
11. Dual range rear end
12. Hitch and tow package
13. Recliners
14. Trash compactor
15. Power step

16. Built-in TV's (bedroom and living room)
17. Built-in VCR system
18. Built-in vacuum system (with outside connection)
19. Lighted wardrobes
20. Pump switch in bathroom
21. Outside water spigot
22. Built-in blender/can opener
23. Black water holding tank flushing system (60+ gal. tank)
24. Patio awning and window awnings
25. Roof rack/ladder
26. Basement model
27. Tile counter tops
28. Tinted windows
29. Clothes hamper
30. Generator
31. Recessed (ducted) air conditioners with heat strips
32. Satellite antenna system
33. Forced air heating
34. Microwave oven
35. Complete range and oven
36. Amplified TV antenna
37. Built-in desk/computer
38. Telephone with external jacks
39. Security (alarm) system
40. Automatic leveling jacks
41. Adequate bedroom drawer space
42. Good use of bedroom wall space
43. Remote control mirrors with defrosters
44. Aluminum wheels
45. Heavy-duty radial tires
46. 100-200 gal. fuel cap
47. 100-gallon fresh water cap
48. 50-60 gallon grey water cap
49. Electronic refrigerator
50. Electronic furnace ignition
51. Electronic water heater
52. Four speed HD transmission
53. CD player and stereo system
54. Ener-genius converter/inverter system
55. AC circuit wired for computer
56. Cellular telephone
57. Base single-sideband CB
58. Docking lights/remote spotlight
59. Deadbolt locks for all entry doors
60. Acoustic ceiling
61. Dinette in the galley
62. Separate living room
63. Large tub and/or shower area
64. Adequate closet space
65. Plumbing and heating ducts clear of cabinet storage space
66. AC outlets in logical places
67. Adequate galley storage
68. Quality carpeting
69. Smoke alarms
70. LP gas detector/alarm
71. Storm windows

Don't be alarmed by the above list. It's only a dream—but since dreams allow you to do anything you'd like, we have dreamed it our way.

10

How Will We Get Around, Once We've Parked Our Home?

"Hold up my goings in Thy paths, that my footsteps slip not."
Psalm 17:5

Travel Modes

Okay, it's settled in your mind. You have now decided that your goal is to become "dyed in the wool" full-timers. You have made the big decision, and thus chosen your personal RV home.

Let's project into the future and find out just what you can expect once you're out there in the RV world.

You have established your very first campsite in your new way of life. The place where you have encamped has many scenic and cultural opportunities to explore, with many sights to see—and they are all several miles apart. It is going to require several days (or possibly even weeks) to explore all of this splendor.

Several questions arise, which must be answered in order for you to fully appreciate the richness of this life and take advantage of the opportunities available:

- How long do you plan to stay in one location?
- Where do you plan to go for groceries and other supplies?
- How do you plan to cover the distance to the nearest market, to see the local sights, to a church or synagogue of your faith, to a local theater, or to a restaurant?

These are things you would do if you were living in a stationary home. Since you will now be living in this home, these questions must be answered, hopefully long before you are in this situation.

Let's discuss some forms of alternate transportation. As we have stated in previous chapters, the particular type of RV you have chosen goes a long way in deciding what this alternate transportation will be.

Travel Trailer and/or Fifth-Wheel

If you have chosen a travel trailer or a fifth-wheel, naturally you may use your tow vehicle for transportation when you are away from your campsite. Many people carry bicycles as an alternate mode of transport (and exercise)—or even motor scooters or motorcycles. These vehicles allow them to leave their tow vehicle attached if they are staying in one area for a short time (Chapter 12 discusses methods for carrying these modes of transport).

Whether it is a pickup truck, van, jeep (or other four-wheel-drive vehicle)—or an automobile outfitted to be the tow vehicle for your travel trailer—you are already equipped with transportation once the trailer is unhitched. If a fifth-wheel is your RV home, the tow vehicle is still your natural choice for transportation.

We have seen some beautiful tow rigs for both the travel trailer and the fifth-wheel. These are made from customized diesel tractors (for the big rigs), vans and pickup trucks. There are several local and national companies whose sole business is to create these specialty vehicles. Some of them are outfitted with extended cabs containing entertainment centers with TV's, stereo CD's, swivel/recliner seats, and bunks and beds. They are designed to allow a whole family to ride together, or to sleep overnight away from the main rig.

NOTE

For those of you thinking about purchasing a large, diesel tractor conversion, and using it as your transportation while not towing, you will find it a bit much to take this rig into traffic for grocery shopping, laundry, and the bank. You may want to consider bringing along an alternate means of transportation if you make this choice.

These vehicles are generally quite pricey—in the $35,000 to $75,000 range—however, we have seen them reasonably priced on the resale market. Of course, as with any purchase of a used vehicle, the buyer must beware, and be prepared to accept someone else's problems.

These vehicles may not be the most economical means of travel when you consider gas mileage, wear-and-tear on your essential tow vehicle, and tire replacement costs.

Motorhome

If you have decided that a Class A or Class C motorhome, a pickup camper, a van conversion or Lo-Profile RV is to be your full-time home, several solutions to the alternate transportation problem are presented to you as well:

- You can just drive your "home" wherever you plan to go. This will do in a pinch. However, the task of unhooking and putting away your breakables—not to mention your gas mileage and size of your rig just to go for a short trip to the grocery store or laundromat—make it an unhandy choice. If it's a quick trip, you can probably go there and come back in alternate transportation in the time it would take to get ready to make the trip in your home.

- However, if you are going to be away for the day (at, for instance, a picnic) and have someone with you who needs to lie down or have clean restroom facilities nearby, you'll be the envy of the crowd. Air shows and visits to places like Disneyland will make you love your RV. You can turn on the generator and start the air conditioner midday for a little rest (and cheaper food) without having to leave the area.

- You can carry bicycles, motor scooters, or motorcycles as discussed in Chapter 12.

- You can plan to tow another (normally smaller, more economical) vehicle behind your home.

Each of these solutions is viable and we have encountered many examples of every resolution. Of course, the way you personally live in and use your RV will determine the method you will employ to get around while stopped or at a campsite. Do you put out chairs, barbecues and rugs every time you camp, or is your campsite spartan and devoid of things that make it look like you've "staked your claim?"

Discussion

Van conversions, pickup campers, and Lo-Profile motorhomes are most often the RVs that people will use as their home and as alternate transportation vehicles. As a rule, these units are so compact that when it is time to go, there is little preparation required to move on.

We have seen these rigs in parking lots and malls all over the country. Many people drive them to church, drive-in movies, swap meets, rallies, and auctions. For the most part, these small rigs fit into almost any normal sized parking spot and you will find them parked in most downtown areas. When we had our first Class C motorhome—a 23' unit—we parked it on Constitution Avenue in downtown Washington, D.C. on the Fourth of July. Talk about a ringside seat for a parade!

We have used our motorhome for major grocery shopping and found it handy simply to bring the cart out to our house in the parking lot, and put the ice cream in the freezer right away. We've seen some surprised looks on the faces of bag-boys when we've asked them to help "push our grocery carts out to our house."

This type of shopping is a normal practice for us as we travel across country, especially when we are between campgrounds.

Bicycles, Motorcycles, Etc.

If your only alternate transportation is a bicycle, motor scooter, or motorcycle, you can imagine how impractical it is to do any large scale grocery shopping. Even traveling a great distance (fifty miles or more) from your campsite will be difficult.

On a bicycle, the average person is limited by the distance s/he can travel and still return to the campsite on the same day. Most people are not willing to stay overnight on a sightseeing outing.

With the motor scooter (or a motorcycle), while it is easier to travel greater distances, inclement weather and fatigue become factors, thus also limiting their range. However, these forms of transportation are very economical, and the bicycle is good for your health.

*Special racks make it easy to carry
your alternate transportation.*

Our Personal Solution

We have found, as have most full-timers in motorhomes, that towing a smaller vehicle behind the motorhome is our best solution. The smaller vehicle is much more economical on fuel, tires, and insurance. It is easier to handle no matter where you must drive, whether downtown in a large city, or into a small tourist resort or Native American village.

Making the Decision

When we made our choice about what we would tow behind our motorhome, we took several items into account:

1. How much money did we have for an alternate vehicle?

2. How did we plan to tow it—all four tires on the ground, on a car caddy, or inside a pull trailer?

3. How did we plan to use it on the road?

4. Would we need to carry anything in the vehicle that wouldn't fit, or that we didn't want in the motorhome (such as tools and other garage-type items)?

5. What type of vehicle did we want—four-wheel drive, mini pickup, small car, or small van?

Our decision was based upon the answers to each of these questions, as follows:

1. We had to pay cash for this vehicle, since we would have no regular income. We decided to buy the best one we could, with the amount of money we had available.

2. We couldn't spend additional money for a tow trailer, with its attendant tires, requiring an additional spare, so we voluntarily limited ourselves to a vehicle with a standard transmission, which we could tow "four down" in neutral. Alternatively, we could have opted for a drive-line disconnector and towed a vehicle with an automatic transmission. However, these units, with installation, are about as expensive as the trailers themselves.

Deanne wants to add something here about fully-enclosed automobile tow trailers. Gene continues to dream of these "portable garages." They could conveniently store tools, and we could buy a small car to use as a towed vehicle, which the trailer would keep clean.

But Deanne says her "warning light flashes." Some situations have forced us to unhook the truck, and she has had to drive it out separately. How would she drive a garage?

Towed garages keep your tools and vehicles clean.

a. A few times we've pulled into a gas station or small parking lot, and found it necessary to back up with our rig. However, when pulling a vehicle with all four wheels down, you cannot back up and properly control the towed vehicle. We've had to unhook the truck. Of course, you soon learn to reconnoiter the situation before entering.

b. Once we were driving up a steep mountain road and our motorhome engine overheated. Had we continued, we may have burned up the engine, trying to pull the RV and the truck up that hill. Again, we had to unhook the truck and drive up separately. In this instance, unloading the small car would have been sufficient to lighten the load on the RV engine, and allow it to pull up the empty trailer.

Gene says that you can install a hitch on your small vehicle and use it to tow your garage in difficult situations. Just keep these problems in mind when considering a pull trailer.

3. We planned to use the vehicle as our alternate transportation when we were stopped in a location for more than one night.

4. We also planned to carry within our towed vehicle all of Gene's tools, toolboxes, and accumulated spare parts with which to maintain the motorhome, all of its systems, and the alternate transportation itself.

5. Thus, we decided that the S-10 pickup we already owned outright was the ideal alternate transportation for us. All we had to do was add a topper, bra and windshield cover to protect the front end of the pickup and we were in business.

Our next choice for an alternate vehicle will probably be a Blazer, Bronco, or some other rough country vehicle that will hold four people. We'll have to pare down our tools, but we've found we don't use most of them anyway. Our bigger frustration has been that when we meet friends with whom we want to go on an outing, we have to drive two vehicles.

Chevrolet has decreed that you couldn't tow this vehicle in the manner we planned—apparently in order to save having to warranty the transmission in case of problems. We have never experienced a problem, nor has anyone else with whom we have come in contact, who is towing one.

We were aware that there would be no warranty on our truck's drive line and transmission, and that it would accumulate miles on the speedometer beyond those on the engine. But it was paid for, ran well, and met all of our needs. Besides, more than worrying about trade-in value, we were concerned with its service to us for as long as it was usable. If you are planning to buy a vehicle for alternate transportation, check with your dealer or manufacturer's representative for the recommended manner in which to tow it.

Planning for a Future Transportation Vehicle

A good plan for the day when you will have to buy another transportation vehicle is to save your money by paying those "unused" monthly truck/automobile payments to your own savings account (if you can, and as money is earned regularly). Thus, when your transport vehicle eventually wears out, there will be funds available to purchase another. We have always thought the best way to buy a vehicle was with our own money, and therefore make payments to ourselves, just as if we were a bank.

How does this work? Buy the vehicle you need and pay for it however you must. When it is paid for, continue to put that same monthly amount into the bank. Then when you have enough to trade up, use your money and your paid-for vehicle as a trade-in, and buy a better vehicle. Continue to save the payments, and repeat this cycle. It's amazing to see how much money you'll save—and it is doubly amazing to see how much money you have really paid for automobiles in the past.

Pros and Cons

One consideration in purchasing an RV is the question of having to maintain more than one vehicle. With a motorhome you have two—the RV and the towed vehicle. With a trailer/fifth-wheel, you only have the tow vehicle. That extra vehicle's added engine tuneups and other requirements, on a limited budget, can be a major part of your determination.

We must admit that while this is a factor, it may justify itself for you when combined with other considerations. For instance:

- The use of the added vehicle will undoubtedly save on fuel, maintenance, insurance, and tire expenses on your RV. Using a bike saves on gas as well as the tow vehicle for any standard-sized trailer unit.

- The longevity of the more expensive RV or tow vehicle will be increased because of the longer periods between required tuneups, overhauls, and repairs.

- Services on the alternate vehicle will generally cost less, and often can be performed by the owner.

Emergencies

We have found that in emergencies, having the extra vehicle has proven to be of inestimable value. We drive for help instead of walking or waiting alongside the road.

Occasionally we like to travel in some out-of-the-way places. It is comforting to know we have a backup system in case the motorhome engine fails or a tire blows.

On our first cross-country trip, we had occasion to be glad for the truck. We experienced battery problems on the motorhome and were unaware of it until after we had stopped on a little side road in the desert for an afternoon siesta.

As we prepared to continue our journey, the motorhome would not click, let alone start. By unhooking the truck and driving it around in front of the motorhome, we could jump-start the motorhome engine. Once it started, it could run, though the battery was too low to start the engine. This enabled us to continue on until we could find a place to buy a new battery.

It was inconvenient to unhook the truck and handle this situation in the desert heat. However, it certainly was easier than taking the house battery out of a fifth-wheel and using that as a jump-starter, or waiting for help to come on that desert road.

We have heard many pros and cons concerning each of these different kinds of full-time RV homes and the types of alternate transportation methods. What we have discovered is that every person we have talked to has had their own reasons for doing it their way, and it works—for them. Ability, availability, under-standing, opportunity, money, and outright preference are all factors in this decision. With the many variables, we are all bound to make different choices that will competently suit each situation.

11

CAN WE LIVE WITH OUR KIDS, OR TAKE PETS IN OUR RV HOME?

"Train up a child in the way he should go:
and when he is old, he will not depart from it."
Proverbs 22:6

"A righteous man regardeth the life of his beast . . ."
Proverbs 12:10

In our travels across the country, we have met many young families who live full-time in their RVs. It is a real and feasible alternative for a family with children still at home.

Also, more than half the people we have met have a pet of some kind living with them in their RV. We offer the following information to help in caring for your children and pets while you travel. Also, to provide some help for locating schools and/or courses available to full-timers, or, for that matter, anyone else who wants education without having to attend a school.

Providing Accommodations for
Full-Timing With Children

It is only common sense to always have enough seating for every member of the family. When traveling with youngsters, you must also provide for their short attention spans and make provisions for keeping them occupied. Whole areas of toy stores are set aside for travel ideas with games, toys, and puzzles for traveling youngsters. Make provisions for allowing your family some movement—and give them snacks and a place for naps.

Safety Preparations and Precautions

Most states now require that the rig be equipped with seat belts for all occupants (in motorhomes, vans, and in all tow vehicles). In most states, occupants may travel in a towed fifth-wheel trailer or in a pickup camper. However, no state allows passengers to occupy a moving travel trailer.

Parents should establish rules concerning moving about within the vehicle while it is in motion. We had to establish just such a rule for ourselves after a mishap that, luckily, was not more costly in injury or money.

Dangerous Move, Folks!

This accident occurred when Deanne had to meet a deadline on a book she was writing for a client, and we also had to arrive at a given place by a certain date. We own a portable computer, which enabled Deanne to write as we traveled. This usually isn't a problem, unless we travel through a city and have to contend with traffic.

She was concentrating on research papers that she had dropped on the floor—and was paying no attention to our surroundings. Suddenly, as she stood to retrieve the papers, the traffic in front required that Gene stop—quickly! This action resulted in a backward fall for Deanne, two broken ribs, much pain, a terrified driver (and dog), papers everywhere, a broken cabinet, a shaken-up computer, and a new rule: "No getting up out of your seat while traveling in city traffic." Deanne did meet her deadline—but had to sit in a chair with pillows around her to use the computer every day—and we arrived where we needed to be on time. We also learned a valuable lesson, relatively cheaply. We are now passing it on to you, maybe not free, but again, relatively cheaply.

Education

The question for young families is: "How can we go on the road? We still have our children at home with us. The law requires that we keep them in school, and, of course, we want them to have the best possible education."

These are important considerations, and for most people, will preclude any thought of attempting this nomadic way of life. However, for the more adventurous, there are many ways to ensure that your children will receive a good education (one that cannot even be obtained in a classroom) and still allow you to travel and live full-time in your RV.

Home Teaching Method

Today there are several popular and up-to-date companies that provide curriculum, lesson plans, and certification of grades for home schooling. These lessons normally are designed to allow the parent to oversee the studies of their students/children. The *Home Education Resource Guide*, as shown in Appendix D, is a good, comprehensive guide to curriculums, correspondence schools, legal information, and school books for the parent-educator. You can obtain this publication from a local library.

If correspondence school is your choice, the University of Nebraska-Lincoln may help you with one of their correspondence study programs. Their address is shown in Appendix B.

Correspondence with the providing company on grading lessons and keeping records is relatively simple for the RV traveler, but it will require adherence to a schedule of sorts to allow for receiving mail regularly. Certification of types of disciplines studied and credits earned toward graduation are available from these companies to allow reentry into the public school system, or for college use.

The home teaching method requires habitual discipline by the entire family, as proper periods of instruction and areas for study must be made a matter of family priority. In the confines of an ordinary RV, it will require cooperation by every member of the family to observe the rules and allow time and space for the development of good study habits for the student(s). The lessons must fit into the schedule of the parents, and the family must create a quiet study time.

Of course, home schooling has some advantages that are not normally available to the student in public schools:

- The children can be given more individual attention for those subjects that are not easy for them. Also, they can study at their own pace. This is an advantage for either the slower learner or the one who grasps a concept quickly. The slow learner has the opportunity to understand a lesson completely before moving on to the next one. For the quick learners, the ability to forge on to new things and ideas will keep them from the boredom that often exists in regular classrooms.

- Can you imagine the thorough teaching that a child would receive in visiting the sites where the Civil War took place, or museums that house the history of inventions such as the cotton gin, airplanes and automobiles? They might even get the chance to talk personally to the experts on special subjects. These scholars might enjoy the opportunity to share their knowledge with children who can visit them when other young people are in school.

Many people have reported that this type of schooling has brought their family closer together, due to the necessary cooperation and reliance upon each other in order for home schooling to be a success.

The home schooling method requires dedication by the whole family to ensure that the children's education is complete. However, it is not the only educational option available to full-timers and their families.

Caution

> *Be sure to check with your home state's laws on home schooling. Some states may require that you pass a tutor's exam to qualify as an instructor to your own children. They may also stipulate that you submit your particular chosen curriculum for certification.*

Private Schools

Many people place their children in private boarding schools. The reasons for this are variable, and have no bearing on the decision to live in an RV and travel during the school year.

Boarding schools provide the children the best in private education, while allowing them to travel with their parents during the remainder of the year. For certain children and parents' occupations, these arrangements can be most beneficial to the entire family. However, just like the home schooling arrangement, private boarding schools are not for everyone.

Use Of The Public School System

To understand this concept fully, it must be remembered how we defined a "full-timer" in Chapter 1; i.e., anyone, group, or family who lives wholly in an RV for an extended period during the year can be considered a full-timer.

The public school teaching method is probably used by full-timers more than any other. The reasons are varied and numerous: They didn't know that there was any other way to educate their children; they cannot afford any other method; they like the school or system where their children attend; their lengths-of-stay in an area due to jobs held by the parents are long enough to allow the children to get to stay for one-half, or sometimes all of one school year.

Whatever the reasons, the public school system is an alternative to be used as follows:

- Because they are free, the parents can simply choose a state and a city (or rural school district) where they want to send their children for schooling.

- They can then determine the particular school in that district where they plan for the children to attend.

- They can locate a campground that is near their school of choice and register their children for attendance.

- Always, they must be prepared to defend their right to allow their children to attend the public school system.

Many people in the local communities fail to realize that RV travelers are paying for the schools in the same manner as the people of the community who are home and apartment owners/renters. Just as the owner of the house or apartment must pay property taxes, the owner of the RV Park (or local trailer park) must pay property taxes. It is from these taxes that the school systems are funded.

Also, every public school (and certain private schools) receives federal and state funds based upon the head count in the school. The children of full-timers are also counted in this number, and this helps to bring additional revenue into the school.

Cost of Education

Private boarding schools are generally more costly than the at-home curriculum, but tend to offer much the same in the way of individualized teaching.

We recommend that you check with the local school board and library system for further information on education.

Providing Accommodations for
Full-Timing With Pets

Many folks keep pets in their stationary homes. They provide companionship, and are objects of affection who can double as a learning tool for youngsters in developing a sense of responsibility for their care.

Most families thus derive a great deal of joy and satisfaction from keeping their pets when they begin to travel. We kept our dog, Brandy, because he had grown up with us. We felt he was worth the trouble of finding out if we could all live together in cramped quarters before we gave him to someone else. His well-being was always a concern to us, however—as we will explain. We have since found some wonderful people in our travels who fell in love with him and asked to have him live with them in their stationary home. It seemed best for us (because we work away from the motorhome so much) and for him and his new owners. We can't say it wasn't a hard decision—or that it would be the best one for anyone else.

Although this decision may seem harsh to some, we decided that our dog was still a pet. We didn't want to live our lives for our pets any more than we wanted to live them for our things. We hope that if you're a pet lover you don't stop reading here, deciding that we're heartless people. We really aren't. It was a decision that caused a great deal of stress, but in the end, we feel it was best for all of us.

The "Horn-Honking" Terrier

We've met some "personality pets" along the way. One who comes to mind entertained us one afternoon—a little terrier who was left behind in his master's RV.

We were all standing outside talking when we heard a horn honk several times. The man we were speaking with turned his head toward the noise, and the honking ceased. A few minutes later it began again, and again the man turned to look. Soon we realized that it was his dog honking the horn. He was evidently upset at not being invited outside to join us.

Watching carefully, we saw through the windshield that the dog was jumping up onto the dashboard and honking the horn with his front paws. When his master would look at him, he would jump down, run over to the door, and wait a minute. If the door did not open, he would return to the dashboard and repeat the process. What an innovative companion.

It's Your Choice

If you choose to take your pet along, there are several considerations you will want to remember:

- Take along all of your pet's important papers/belongings (pedigree information, inoculation records, any special medications and/or prescriptions) and in the cases of lost, stolen, or wandering pets, pictures and any other proof of ownership and identification. A veterinarian can apply a tattoo of your social security number or any other identifying number. Recently available are the new micro-chip implants; ask your local veterinarian about them.

- Be prepared to meet their special needs as your own: A different veterinarian, foods that may not be available in different parts of the country, etc.

- You must set aside room for your pet's toys and food, and a place for them to rest, eat, and exercise. Since space is valuable, you will want to consider whether you have it to spare. In our case, we eventually had to take up the carpeting in the galley and replace it with tile. Our dog's eating and lapping of water, even on the little mat under his bowls, took their toll on that area.

Kinds of Pets that Make Good Travelers

There are several kinds of animals that full-timers have successfully taken with them (and this list is not intended by any means to be exhaustive): Dogs, cats, skunks, birds, snakes, fish, and horses are all examples of the animals we have seen in our travels. We are sure there are people traveling with animals that we have never even heard of—let alone would consider sharing close quarters with. However, no matter what type of pet you have, it will be your responsibility to oversee the animal's health, welfare, and safety as you travel with it.

Safety Preparations and Precautions

Some states require that animals traveling inside a vehicle be constrained either in a safety harness or within a cage. They contend—and rightly so—that an animal that is permitted to roam loose in the vehicle can become frightened and interfere with the driver and inadvertently cause an accident.

*   *Four-Legged Passengers.* We recommend that you keep your four-legged pet in a safety device such as a cage, especially as you travel in congested traffic areas. The stop-and-go traffic tends to make animals very nervous, and sudden movements or sharp noises can frighten them. A frightened pet may tend to run to his master and try to get on his/her lap, causing a dangerous situation, especially when major concentration is required.

*   *Birds.* If you travel with birds, you will probably want to keep them in their cages as you travel, for much the same reason. A bird flying into the face of the driver can indeed be distracting. Of course, there may be the other obvious reasons too: We have only known one person—Gene's Great Uncle Archie—who successfully potty-trained his parakeet. Uncle Archie didn't travel in an RV, though; he lived in a tiny apartment with the bird (the resale value of your RV might be protected by heeding this advice).

- *Fish.* If you travel with tropical fish, you probably won't have to worry too much about them flying into the driver's face. But you must carefully follow the requirements for your type of fish. If you plan to travel with anything more than the hardy guppy or goldfish, you've probably already gained full knowledge of the special needs of your chosen species.

  Generally, though, you must provide a tank or fishbowl that will survive the twists and turns of the road without spillage. It must furnish proper temperature control of the water and aeration for the fish's well-being.

  Aquariums will have to be solidly mounted and not overfilled. You'll have to anchor down decorative items within the tank or they will tend to move about. ("Look out, Phoebe! Here comes the sunken treasure chest, and dodge that flying rock!").

  While traveling, the water will probably become cloudy from the stirred-up sediment at the bottom of the tank. An under-gravel filter system may not prove as beneficial as would an external filtration system.

- *Reptiles (Terrariums).* When you travel with snakes or other reptiles, the most practical means of caging them is with a terrarium (dry aquarium). You'll have to securely anchor all rocks and larger items to prevent injury or harm to the pet and the tank itself. However, a terrarium will allow you to visually check on the animal as you travel.

Important RV-Pet Facts

When you travel with any kind of animal, you must be aware of the dangers (to the animals) and the drawbacks (to your travel freedom).

A problem you will no doubt be faced with at some time is your need to leave for a day or two; perhaps to go to Disneyworld, attend a seminar or important social function; anything that precludes taking your pet with you. What do you do with Fido, Tabby or Phoebe?

The inside of any RV will tend to become extremely hot very quickly (120 to 140 degrees Fahrenheit in the summer); even during the milder parts of the year the temperature can reach deadly heights. Therefore, it is not recommended (or even allowed in many campgrounds) that you leave your pet unattended inside an RV.

While many people do leave them inside with the air conditioner running, in a power failure, the temperature will be uncontrolled. Power failures are quite common in campgrounds, due to the changing load conditions as people come and go. Also, many older campgrounds are not as modern as the RVs they serve, having been built twenty to thirty years ago for the RV units of that era. This means that the old 15-amp power connection cannot carry the continuous load of a modern air conditioner.

"Brandy"

When we first began to travel full-time, taking our little Sheltie Brandy along with us, he was the best traveler. We truly enjoyed the two years that we spent with him on the road.

However, because of noise problems and the danger of pets biting curious children, danger to the pet itself from wild animals or strays, or damage to the site by digging or chewing up plants, most campgrounds prohibit leaving your pet unattended outside the RV. We had a couple of experiences that helped to underscore the importance of this rule.

The Rules

As we traveled, we discovered our rules and their rules, and the reasons behind each of them:

Rule 1. Too many pet owners are too lazy to properly clean up after their animals and leave the telltale signs at your doorstep. Therefore, as a pet owner, most parks reserve a place for your RV in the "pet area"—no grass, no bushes, no fun—and generally no clean environment.

Brandy

Rule 2.   Our ability to be free to work or travel away from the
           RV was greatly limited. We found that we had to bend
           the rules just to be able to go buy groceries. No
           grocery store allows you to bring your pet.

We either had to tie Brandy up and leave him outside (for the
one to two hours the trip to the store took) or leave him inside
with the air conditioner running. Both solutions were technically
wrong, but we found that there was no alternative, and we took
our chances (actually Brandy's chances, as the following will
illustrate):

Arizona and the coyotes. One spring morning in Arizona, we
left Brandy on his tether outside the RV while we went shopping.
We had done it several times before, and thought nothing of it for
the short time we were to be gone. On the way back to the camp-

ground, we observed a pair of coyotes crossing the road as they left the camp area.

Coyotes are notorious for attacking and killing pets. Just the week before, we had heard a story of one having attacked and carried off a poodle as the owner was out walking it. Our hearts were in our throats as we approached our campsite, preparing ourselves for the worst. When we arrived, we found Brandy sleeping contentedly in the shade of the RV, unaware of any danger. Needless to say, we never left him outside alone in that campground again.

Florida and the 'gators. Another time, in Florida shortly after some heavy rains, we were staying in an RV resort park along a small river. Having the same shopping needs, we left Brandy outside again. This was a residential park with mostly permanently set up park models so we thought surely there would be no danger for him. However, that night we heard that an alligator had come out of that very river due to the high water from the rain and carried off a dog. Poor Brandy—something was always waiting to eat him!

Fortunately, we learned some reasons for these "harsh" rules without mishap.

Rule 3.   Some campgrounds do have boarding facilities (or can recommend a local kennel) for the ordinary cat or dog (maybe even for your bird). If your pet is exotic, forget it.

This, then, becomes an added expense that you must contend with if you choose to travel with your pet. Any frustration must be weighed against the satisfaction that you receive from the love and companionship of your pet.

The choice is yours to make and we can only commend you for that choice, either way. There is room for all of us on the road. All we have to say about the matter is: Be a responsible pet owner; clean up after it, make sure it doesn't disturb your neighbors with barking or other noises, and provide for its safety and protection. Your pet can live a long and happy life with you on the road. By the way, Brandy is delighted, in his new home, to find he doesn't need to "mark his territory" anew every day.

Horses

In the west we have encountered a few folks who travel with their horses. We do not intend to cover in detail all of the requirements of this endeavor. If you plan to travel with horses, you should contact the Western Horsemen group for information on the means and campgrounds that make provisions for pets of this kind. We have listed their address in Appendix D.

12

WHAT CAN WE DO FOR FUN?

"Behold, how good, and how pleasant it is for brethren
to dwell together in unity!" (Oneness of mind . . .)
Psalm 133:1

Recreational Activities

Transporting "Recreational" Vehicles

There are no limits to the imaginations of the full-timers we have met. Whatever the endeavor, they will devise a means to take their recreational vehicles with them.

Whether they opt for the desert—using jeeps, dunebuggies, or motorcycles; yearn for the lakes and seashores—to use their boats, waterskis, fishing poles, and Jet Skis; or make tracks to the mountains and/or North Country—to use their snowmobiles and snow skis, they will find a way to take their means of enjoyment on top of, behind, or under their RV or tow vehicle.

Travelers can purchase almost all recreational vehicles with their own specially designed transport trailers. Also, the old standby utility trailer can be made over, redesigned, or added to, to make it into a carrier for our adult toys. See the information in Chapter 8 pertaining to the Weekend Warrior for transporting your recreational vehicles.

A jeep or dunebuggy is sometimes substituted for the towed vehicle, and thus becomes the alternate transportation vehicle, as well as the play vehicle. This is most common for motorhome users. These ingenious fun seekers also employ racks, ramps, and special carriers. Whatever the activity, someone has a method to take the vehicle to the event. Bicycle racks by the dozens have been designed and sold to the industry: bolt-ons, clamp-ons, weld-in-place, car-tops, and every other possible style—in order to take along their two-wheeled conveyances—are pressed into service.

Exploration

Dunebuggies, jeeps, motorcycles, and even bicycles allow us to explore the regions that we visit. The primary reason to take these vehicles with us is to follow all the trails that can lead us to the hidden beauty of an area, or to lost ghost towns or other types of ruins. Some people just like to ride their bicycle or motorcycle down an unfamiliar trail merely to observe what's to see along the way, or to find what lies at the end of it.

Full-time RV adventurers have unlimited possibilities.

Full-timers are also fond of the many hiking trails to explore in the National Parks and Forests, and the state and private preserve trails. Many people combine one or more means of getting around in the wilderness with a desire for hunting in the fields, or fishing in the streams and lakes they encounter.

Passive Activities

Bird-watching, photography, painting (in oils, watercolors, or sketching) can also be included in these activities. Often the full-timer can even transform one or more of these skills into a profitable endeavor. Paintings and sketches are always popular items to sell in campground bazaars. Many nature, camping, and travel magazines eagerly purchase freelance photography.

New Friends

A full-timer's lifestyle makes it easy to find and cultivate new friends. New campgrounds, churches, garage sales, swapmeets, and exciting new cities and villages are all places that the average person only dreams of visiting. Wherever the full-timer goes, he or she is the one of interest to the local people. Full-timers always have stories of places and events that are only mentioned in the news or in magazines. The full-timer is someone "who has been there" and can give the local folks firsthand information. People are always curious about the stranger in their midst, and if you are friendly and willing to share, new friends are but a handshake and friendly greeting away.

Places

New localities (towns, villages, mountains, deserts, farms, or ranches); National Forests, Parks, and Monuments; state parks, recreational areas; monuments; and areas of local history are not merely interesting things to read about, but are now available for you to discover.

The full-timer has the time and the opportunity to really explore this country with its myriad of historical and natural wonders. Our personal favorite is finding old, abandoned houses that are falling into ruin. There we can take pictures and imagine what these houses were like when the laughter of children filled their rooms. We can wander through (if "No Trespassing" signs are not evident) and look for hidden treasures. We search for old newspapers and magazines, and examine life as it was "back then."

Old barns are also full of history, and afford an insight into the unique ways that work has been accomplished. Seeking out these places, and talking to the owners, or anyone aware of their past, is a wonderful way to get a firsthand education in local history. Not to mention—again—new friends.

Many farms and ranches around the country welcome us with open arms for the camaraderie and the work we can do for them. While not all farms and ranches are equipped to hire help and provide room and board, many of them have a place to park and allow you to "plug-in." Many a good friendship (and financial partnership) can be cultivated through these arrangements. Full-timers are free to work as long as there is work available. We are independent enough to have the freedom to move on when the work is done. As with the parting of friends, there need be no guilt or hard feelings as may be between the parting of hired-hand and employer.

Many private "dude" ranches have facilities to allow full-timers to participate in their programs. These are the places where you can learn much about the life on the great ranches of the Old West. If you are knowledgeable about this life, or have had experience in ranching or farming, this may prove to be another possible source of income.

Food and Culture

Local restaurants, theaters, and museums are only the beginnings for exploring the culture of a locality. A typical local restaurant (not a McDonald's or other chain) will give you a feel for the people in the area. What you find on the menu will tell much about the people and their lifestyles.

Local restaurant owners tend to feature the types of food popular in that area. Don't assume that because you know the name of a particular dish, you have eaten it before. The method of cooking, as well as its ingredients, can vary greatly from region to region.

Does the town or city you are visiting have a theater or stage production company? These events provide much entertainment, both in the way of attendance and in participation. If you are so inclined, the locals may employ your talents to help in their theater production. Many talents and skills are required to make a success of these events, and the full-timer may just have the needed ones. He or she may also have more time to devote to the production.

Concerts, movies, and seminars are also gratifying events for expanding the mind and widening our horizons. A concert, where they are playing your choice of music, is always a good place to meet like-minded people. Seminars that teach, and allow you to expand your personal knowledge, are also good places for cultivating friendships. Or have you thought of giving one yourself? People always want to hear how we live on the road. See J & D Associates' seminar "Living the Full-Time RV Life" on the last page of this book. "Have you seen such and such a movie"—and the following conversation—is a great icebreaker for meeting new people.

Face it folks—when it comes down to it, we are gregarious creatures at the core. All of our endeavors are to elicit approval or friendship from those with whom we come in contact. Full-timers who have fun are those people who have learned to like themselves, and to look for the good things about those they meet. What great fun it is to find ways and places to meet these people!

13

WHAT DO WE NEED TO KNOW ABOUT OUR RV'S SYSTEMS?

*"If any of you lack wisdom, let him ask of God,
that giveth to all men liberally, and upbraideth not;
and it shall be given him."* **James 1:5**

We all know that a house consists of walls, doors, windows, a floor, and a roof—all making up a type of box in which we find shelter and comfort. This box is serviced by water, sewer, electricity, gas, heating, and optional cooling systems—all available for our comfort, cooking, eating, and bathing requirements.

Included are refrigerators, stoves, storage areas such as cabinets and pantry, and bathing and toilet features. This is merely a partial listing of the various systems and appliances that help to make this box into a modern house that we call a home.

At some point in time, we have all been required to service one or more of these systems or appliances (or at least locate someone else who could). Just as living in a house requires this attention to make it function, the systems and appliances within an RV demand similar attention.

Consequently, no book of this kind can ignore the obvious necessity of introducing you to those areas and basic steps required for their proper maintenance (if any).

General Unit Construction

The construction of an RV is similar to that of a conventional house, except for the types of materials used. While the basic RV unit does not approach the size of an ordinary house, no ordinary house is built to withstand the constant stress of moving (up and down as well as twisting) along a roadway. All of this stress is required of the construction used in your RV, and it must withstand these forces at modern freeway speeds!

Whether your RV is a trailer or a motorhome, the foundation for it is a pair of parallel steel beams (the size and strength dictated by the size of the RV). The framework for all modern RVs is constructed of wood, aluminum, or steel (or some combination of all three). The two most common types of outside wall coverings in use today are aluminum sheeting and various fiberglass materials.

Because of the stresses it undergoes, your RV will require frequent inspection for loose or broken fasteners, scratches, cracks, dents, blisters and water leaks. This inspection will compel you to go under, around, on, and sometimes even inside for a closer look. Make a note of anything suspicious, and either fix it or have it checked by an expert as soon as possible.

Insulation

None of the RV manufacturers belonging to RVIA (Recreational Vehicles Industries Association) build a rig that is not at least partially, if not fully, insulated. However, there is no standard for how much insulation is required. Generally, the units fabricated in the colder sections of the United States or in Canada are found to have the most insulation.

We have learned that, typically, the area with the least amount of insulation is the floor. This is not true if the unit of choice is a basement model, however. In the non-basement model, it is important to verify that there is shielding between the metal pan under the floor and the exhaust system that may run near this floor. Radiant heat from the mufflers and tailpipes may be hot enough to melt the solid foam core of the floor structure in that area. We have had to replace the entire floor (from the manifolds to the end of the tailpipes) due to this oversight by the manufacturer.

Roof

The roof is probably the most overlooked area when an RV is being considered for purchase (this is true for a prospective stationary home as well). It is also the most frustrating when it presents us with problems. After all, "It don't leak if it ain't rainin', and who wants to work in the rain to fix it?" Thus, it seems that we all tend to ignore the potential problem until it is too late.

After the purchase of three different types of RVs, we have established some checkpoints we use in looking at the roof of a potential RV. These are checkpoints we recommend you consider while inspecting your prospective unit:

- Be very wary of any unit that has a perfectly flat roof; there is no slope for allowing the water runoff, and it will tend to puddle around the roof vents and the air conditioner. We surely wish we had had this advice when we purchased our units.

- Look for a roof with no seams on the top edge (where the walls and the roof meet). It is better to have the roof overlap the walls if possible.

- Look for a new type of roofing material that is one-piece rubber covering, guaranteed to last for many years. Remember, of course, if you have vents and an air conditioner, there will be seams and holes where they come through the roof. Check the integrity of those seams.

- If there is a ladder up to the roof, make sure that the roof has been reinforced to allow overhead storage. Many trailers have the ladder, but have very limited, if any, reinforcement.

- Determine what you will want to store (spare tire/wheel, ladder or poles, etc.) so you can decide what size of storage unit (pod) you might need to buy, and if it will fit on the roof of this RV.

Windows and Doors

"Holes" (windows and doors) need to be cut into the walls of this box and filled with glass. These make our box on wheels a place for our comfort—and keep out the weather while we stay inside and watch it. Somehow, one or more of these holes need to be opened to allow us in, and then closed to keep out the weather, not to mention uninvited guests like hungry insects or burglars.

There are many manufacturers of windows and doors who sell their wares to the RV industry. Some are initially very expensive, and others initially very cheap. The doors and windows that cause the most problems eventually are almost invariably the cheaper ones. They tend to warp, split, bind, leak, and even break after a few flexes of the rig as it goes down the road. It is very annoying to travel several hundred miles down a twisting, turning, bumping highway—towing or driving your RV rig—and find that you need to readjust or repair the door to gain entrance into your home.

After traveling for about a year, we had a major water leak around our living room window during a rainstorm in Alabama. A closer inspection revealed that the entire window was only attached to the motorhome with four little screws. The balance of the screws (thirty) were either broken or non-existent. Thank heaven we had that leak, or our window could have flown out, causing major damage. Some problems are blessings in disguise.

Doors that won't open or stay in adjustment or windows that won't slide—or leak when it rains—are quite prevalent with some units. Our advice is: be very demanding and ask your dealer for the best in his line. Have him show you the difference.

The best types of windows and doors are radiused. One continuous piece of aluminum forms the frames of these units, which are rounded at the corners. Because they are radiused at the upper corners, they do not tend to change into parallelograms and bind, as do rectangular doors with mitered or "squared-off" corners.

Also, look for units with "jalousie" type of windows. These consist of multiple horizontal panes that crack out like venetian blinds. These windows allow for maximum ventilation while keeping out water from an unexpected rain. Granted, they aren't easy to clean, but you may decide that their serviceability outweighs the occasional cleaning problem. Watch out here, too; the cheap ones allow dirt to come inside on a dusty trail or windy day.

One area that is neglected in the RV industry is the provision for insulating the windows. None of the manufacturers we have met even provide for the installation of storm windows on their RVs. There are at least two aftermarket manufacturers who produce insulated windows for RVs. Their windows are very expensive, double-pane glass, and are custom-made for each individual unit. If you spend a great deal of time in cold country, though, they may be worth the price.

Water Systems

Water—the very sustainer of life. Especially as we in modern America know it. Clean food, clean clothes, clean homes, clean bodies, and clean automobiles.

Washing, scrubbing, cooking, and even drinking; all these activities are made possible because of the ready availability of water through modern plumbing systems.

Almost all of us are accustomed to water available at the turn of a tap or press of a button. It has been a way of life—always there, lots and lots of water—cold water, hot water, right where we want it, right when we need it. As children we learn to wash our hands before we eat, after we eat, after we flush, when we get up, and before we go to bed. "Rinse that glass out; put that in the laundry; wash the dishes; wash the clothes; wash the windows; wash the car; now go wash your hands." Is it any wonder that we take water for granted? This is a life-long habit that can be the "back breaker" for the full-time boondocker.

Water Quantity and Quality

As a full-timer you will begin to think about the water you use, especially as you travel and find yourself between campgrounds that will provide you with full hookups. This is when you will have to remember that what you carry with you is all you've got.

The size of the fresh water tank will be the limitation on your water usage until you can get back to another source of water.

Filters

You also become responsible for the quality of the water you carry. You must consider where you obtain water and determine if it should be filtered, or if it *can* be filtered; and you must maintain your filters so that they can function as required. To believe the advertising is to believe that there are as many types of filters as there are RVs on the road. However, the good news is that only three basic types of filters are available. The charcoal type filter removes odors and tastes. The sediment filter removes suspended particles from the water (this includes the micron filter, which removes all particles greater than its micron rating). Lastly, the reverse osmosis filter, which claims to offer the purity of distilled water. However, it is very costly, slow and—we think—removes all flavor or taste from the water as well.

From our own experience, it is best to fill your fresh water tank only from a known good source. We recommend that you look at it, taste it, and approve of it yourself before filling your tank. Also, use a whole-house combination filter consisting of one each of the charcoal and the sediment types in tandem. Put the sediment filter in front of the charcoal type. Use the combination to supply water to your RV system and even to fill your fresh water tank from known good sources.

You may want to put a micron filter on the supply line to your ice maker if you have one, and to a drinking water faucet at the sink in the galley. These great little filters will make sure that there are no "floaties" in your drink or ice cubes.

Potable Water

It seems unnecessary to discuss the difference between non-potable water and clean drinking water. However, one morning when we were out for a walk in a California campground, we noticed that one camp trailer had their fresh water hose hooked up to the non-potable, emergency fire department water bib. The man was outside, busily setting up his campsite, so we asked him if he was aware that he was hooked up to the non-potable water source. In this campground, which did its own sewage processing, the fire department lines used this reclaimed water.

He seemed a little confused, but thanked us. As we walked away, we heard him say, "Nancy, whatever non-potable water is—throw out the coffee!"

Water Heaters

Your stationary home was connected to the city utilities and a seemingly endless supply of clean (by chemical analysis anyway), sparkling (that's what the commercials say), clear (if you overlook the "floaties" in it) water. You didn't have to think about how you used water, or how much of it you were using. You had access to a thirty, forty, or fifty gallon hot water heater, and could stand in the shower and let all of that hot, relaxing water rinse your tension down the drain.

As an RV dweller, though, be advised that most RVs will

have only a six gallon hot water heater. The more expensive bus-style rigs occasionally offer a ten gallon unit, but six gallon tanks have become a standard size. The recovery time is fairly reasonable. With a "shut-off" shower head, most people can take a decent shower (ten to fifteen minutes) without using all of the hot water.

Cold Weather Preparations

The necessity for preparing your full-time RV for cold weather is quite different from the advice you will read in most RV books and magazines. When you live full-time in an RV, it will always be heated inside, as was your stationary home. You will have to protect the incoming water supply line, the holding tanks, and the waste valves from freezing. This is absolutely the best reason we can find for the basement models that are now available. Almost without exception, the semi-heated basement houses these tanks and valves.

For any type of RV, you may simply disconnect and drain the incoming water supply line to prevent freezing during the night or on colder days. You will then have to use the fresh water tank and the pump system whenever you need water during that period. We advise you to always keep this tank at least partially full.

When it is necessary to refill the fresh water tank, drain any water from the fill hose before stowing it after use. If you leave water in it, the water can freeze, making the hose unusable until it is thawed out.

We've found a method that allows us to keep the fresh water hose connected in mild winter areas. Using electrical heat tape, we wrap the entire hose. We then place foam heater line insulators, which come in four-foot lengths in ½, ¾, and 1-inch diameters, over the heat tape. The water line will still be operable at all temperatures above zero degrees Fahrenheit. Duct tape seals the seams where the foam insulators come together and around the ends of the hose connections. Most campgrounds have 15 amp outlets in the same box as the 30 amp RV outlet; these are very handy to plug in the heat tape without affecting the RV's power source.

As we stated earlier, a basement model will preclude having to worry about preparing the gray and black water holding tanks and the associated valves for cold weather. There are generally heater ducts running into and through the basement area. These will maintain the temperature in the basement at a point above freezing in most areas of the country.

If you do not have a basement model, you can protect these valves and tanks best in freezing weather by keeping them empty. We have tried using heat tapes on the tanks and valves, but have had limited success. Perhaps, if the tanks were coated with a spray-on foam insulation after having the heat tape attached, it would prove to be more effective. If you find that you must still use the tanks in cold weather, you can pour antifreeze into the tank to protect the valves. We use a gallon or two of windshield washer fluid to act as an antifreeze.

Waste Holding Tanks

Recommended/Required Uses

Since the late 1970's, the law has required RVs to have a minimum of two waste holding tanks. One tank is reserved to catch sink, shower, and lavatory water (the "gray water" holding tank). The other tank is directly connected to the toilet and is designated as the "black water" holding tank.

Dumping Practices

Due to water scarcity in some states, the dumping of gray water directly into the ground is allowed. This practice is not recommended unless permission is asked and granted. The basic reason for not dumping indiscriminately is that unless you are familiar with the area, you may be dumping your gray water right over a shallow well or into the run-off for a pond or creek. The bacteria from your gray water should not be allowed to enter these fresh water sources.

Although dumping your gray water well away from such areas may be permissible, it is always the most environmentally safe to use a designated and approved dumpsite every time you dump.

Warning

> *You should never dump the black water tank anywhere but into a properly designated and approved dumpsite, through a sewer hose.*

This is a most important rule in order to prevent spreading of disease and harming of the environment. *Always* use your sewer hose when dumping the black water tank and clean up any spillage after you dump. One of the most disgusting and contemptuous sights we ever saw in our years of camping was watching a person pull up to the dumpsite as close as he could, and then just open the dump valve. Deanne says we should add a special scripture here, which is most appropriate: John 11:39 ". . . Lord, by this time he stinketh . . ." Amen to that!

Many states have removed, or taken out of service, the RV dumpsites that were planned or constructed at the roadside rest areas, simply because of this degrading and dangerously wanton act by unscrupulous and uncaring persons. We can't call them RV'ers, because no RV'er would even consider such an act!

While we are on the subject of holding tanks, it is appropriate to mention the way to use your holding tanks during an extended stay in a campground. Often we see people with both of their dump valves open, without realizing how an RV sewer system functions.

In a stationary home, the sewer system is connected to a series of pipes. These carry all of the waste away in a stream of water (approximately two to six gallons with each flush). The RV system does not use a large volume of water to carry away such sewage. It uses one to two quarts of water to carry the waste directly down into the tank. Thus, when dumping, accumulated water in the tank is required to flush the waste material out of it.

If the valve is left open continuously, there is not enough water used with a single flush to carry away the solids. Thus, the tank will eventually lose its original volume, and it will be difficult to control odor. Most RV holding tank failures are caused by the build-up of these solids in the bottom of the tank.

When we spend any length of time in a campground, we use the holding tanks in the same manner as we do on the road. We keep both valves closed and accumulate the waste water in both tanks. Then, when the black water tank becomes full, we dump it first; then close that valve, and open the valve from the gray tank to rinse out the sewer hose. Even with this practice, we still need to rinse out the tanks quite often using the "jet stream spray head" (See Keeping Those Tanks Sparkling Clean, Chapter 15) to ensure that the gauges continue to operate correctly.

LP Gas

Use Of

The RV uses liquefied propane (LP) gas for the operation of the stove, oven, furnace, refrigerator, and sometimes for lighting. There are also some RVs that have their engines converted to run on LP gas. While LP gas is not as efficient as gasoline, it burns much cleaner. A vehicle that runs on LP gas must run with its LP gas valves open. This is the basis for our belief that it is equally safe to operate the refrigerator on LP while traveling. You must make your own determination, though.

An RV refrigerator operates on LP gas and 120 vac (some can also operate on 12 vdc). However, it has been determined that, for the same setting of the dial in the refrigerator, LP gas is more efficient. Also, by keeping the flame constantly operating in the combustion chamber, we have found that there is less chance for rust to form in the burner area and cause problems there. This advice applies mostly to older models, which have a bulbous boiler area above the burner.

NOTE

> *We have found that a good way to conserve LP gas is to turn the hot water heater off after showers and dishes in the morning. The water will stay fairly hot until we need to turn it on again at night for dinner dishes. Off it goes again until morning, for showers/breakfast dishes, and so on.*

LP Gas Detectors/Alarms

We are truly believers in the use of the LP gas detector/alarm and cannot recommend their use more highly. See the story we told in the Preface regarding this alarm's value to us.

Filling

You must observe a few precautions when it is time to fill your RV's LP gas tanks. The LP tank holds a highly compressed gas that has become liquefied due to the high pressure. All LP tanks are marked with an orientation indicator that tells you how to handle it. Some tanks are designed to be operated only in the vertical position and some are designed as horizontal tanks only. Be careful to use only the properly designated tanks for your RV.

It is very dangerous to get the liquefied gas into the regulator or into the low pressure lines. The tanks should never be over-filled; the proper level for a full tank is 80% of capacity. In some states these tanks can only be filled by weight or after completely emptying the tank, to measure the volume.

Always turn off all appliances during the refill process. To ensure your family's safety, make all of them (and your pets) leave your RV until you have completed the filling process.

*Ground tanks for motorhomes can extend
your stay without inconvenience.*

One disadvantage to using a motorhome as your full-time home is obtaining a fresh supply of LP gas. If you own a trailer (travel trailer or fifth-wheel) you have LP gas tanks or bottles that can be removed from the vehicle and taken to a supplier for a refill.

Ground Tank

Gene decided that we could have the same convenience of a removable tank with an automatic change-over valve on our motorhome. He installed an automatic change-over regulator valve and a five-foot pigtail hose to the existing built-in tank. This allowed us to add a 40 pound ground tank to the LP system and gave us the same convenience that trailer owners have.

When parked, we usually operate from the LP gas in the 40 pound ground tank, leaving the built-in tank in reserve. The automatic change-over valve indicates that the ground tank needs servicing when the red band shows in the window on the valve top. The tank toward which the arrow points is the one requiring service. Then we know that we are operating on the built-in reserve tank and must take the ground tank for a refill. This allows us to go many months before requiring a refill on the built-in tank.

If you plan to stay in one area for any length of time, you can also call a local LP service company and make arrangements for having a large ground tank installed to use with your RV. We have found that LP gas for home use in these tanks is priced differently than it is when you go to a dealer to have your RV tanks filled. Local regulations will apply for this usage.

Electrical Equipment

Modern Americans are almost totally dependent upon electricity to maintain their existence wherever they are. This essential discovery is required to operate the modern gasoline engine (required to move our RVs), to pump water, control and operate refrigerators, heaters and air conditioners, and even to supply light in the darkness.

The modern RV is almost entirely dependent upon electrical power in the many forms that are available. The engine of the motorhome or the towing vehicle requires electricity (from the battery and the alternator) for the ignition system to function. Electricity operates the driving lights, heater, air conditioner, radio, and many other required and convenient devices.

The portion of the RV in which we live is also very dependent upon electricity in its many forms. The lights, entertainment systems, refrigerator (at times), in some rigs the hot water, and even the water supply (via the pump) are dependent upon the power of this modern "miracle" energy.

An RV depends so much on electricity that it has several separate, although related, electrical systems:

- 120-volt AC system

- 12-volt DC systems (vehicular battery and alternator-charging system and the separate RV battery with its converter and charging system)

- (Optional) combination 120-volt AC and 12-volt DC generator

- (Optional) 12-volt DC to 120-volt AC invertor

It is important that RV travelers know the places where electricity is used in their coach. RV users should be aware of the type of electrical energy used in those places (i.e., 120 vac—alternating current, or 12 vdc—direct current, from a battery or other source). Each of these systems, their use, maintenance, and safety precautions is discussed here:

120-Volt AC System (120 VAC)

The alternating current, which is normally available in the duplex outlets found within almost every home in America, is also used in the full-timer's RV. Most of these rigs have AC electrical outlets in the galley and other convenient locations (to the manufacturer's way of thinking, anyway). These supply power to TV's, VCR's, vacuum cleaners, clocks, coffee pots, stereos, hair dryers, and the myriad of other electrical gadgets that are "necessary" to modern man, which must be considered when choosing your rig. Few full-timer's homes lack everything found in this list. Most of us take at least some of them with us for the times when we are connected to shore power or have our generator or invertor operating.

The optional generator is a source of 120 vac power when not connected to shore power. This marvelous device helps make the full-timer feel independent and free from relying upon the rest of the world. Also, the optional invertor is another source of 120 vac power for using many small appliances when not connected to shore power or running the generator. This device allows an RV user to operate one or two of its lower power requirement electrical appliances by converting 12 vdc energy into 120 vac power. As long as the gasoline and fresh water tanks are full, the batteries charged, and the holding tanks empty—with food in the pantry—all systems are ready for self-containment.

Safety

All the safety measures you have been warned of concerning the electrical power used in your stationary home will apply equally to your RV home. The outlets must always be considered "alive"; many RV users travel with their generator operating for the air conditioner, or with the invertor on to make coffee, and nothing should be stuck into them. Watch your children and/or grandchildren!

The most common capacity of the 120 vac system in the RV is 30 amperes. This is the equivalent capacity of two duplex outlets in a stationary house. Keep this value in mind to prevent the inconvenience of having to reset the breakers or replace fuses. The larger fifth-wheels, and the more expensive travel trailers and motorhomes may have dual 30 amp shore-lines or a single 50 amp cable.

With the amperage restrictions as described, many manufacturers do not install an adequate number of outlets in their RVs. They take this measure, we presume, to prevent the possibility of overloading the circuits. This is a mistake; many people will run extension cords and/or put multiple outlet expanders on the few outlets that are supplied. The use of these devices can lead to disastrous situations. Thus, as of this writing, we have installed in our motorhome nine additional outlets.

The extension cord used may not be rated for the appliance plugged into it, and it can become overheated—a potential fire hazard. Also, extension cords running through the RV's close confines may cause you or your children to trip on the cord or accidentally pull an appliance off the stove, cabinet, or table; again, with the potential of fire or injury. Outlet expanders allow too many appliances or other devices to be plugged into a single circuit. If all of the appliances are plugged in simultaneously, the same potential of a fire hazard caused by overheating the wires exists as with the extension cord. However, it exists within the walls of your RV.

With these potential problems in mind, we hope you have the electrical information you need to choose your RV according to your planned requirements. An RV wired with outlets located in the proper places, that does not need extension cords to use your toaster, mixer, or electric skillet, should be your goal. Also your RV should have outlets in all of the living areas where you expect to use electrical devices. It should have outlets in the bathroom, bedroom (you may want to plug a clock/radio, fan, electric blanket, or electric heater), galley, and living room near the gaucho (for lamps, a vacuum cleaner, a fan, or an electric heater).

You must be aware that you cannot use all appliances and electrical devices at once, as you could in your stationary home. Instead, you must learn to ration the use of electrical power. This is because you are limited to 30 amps of power at any time (50 amps in some units) and even less from any one outlet. The process is quite simple, although sometimes irritating. You may have to turn off your air conditioner while using the microwave. Perhaps you will find that you can't operate the toaster while someone is using the hair dryer. You'll soon get the hang of it and will simply ask or investigate which appliance may already be on, before turning on another.

Here is a brief list of those appliances that require higher amperage: The iron, toaster, air conditioner, electric space heater, hair dryer, microwave, toaster oven, electric skillet or crockpot. There is a possibility that you will "kick a breaker" if you attempt to run any more than two of these appliances at once. In your own particular rig, you can experiment and find those appliances that you can run simultaneously with no problem.

Appliance Power Consumption

Food Preparation

Appliance	Watts
Blender	500 - 1,000
Coffee maker	500 - 1,000
Convection oven	1,500-1,700
Dehydrator	250 - 875
Dishwasher	1,000-1,500
Food processor	500 - 750
Frying pan	1,000-1,200
Hot plate/burner	600 - 1,000
Knife	100
Microwave oven	1,000-1,500
Mixer	120 - 250
Oven, separate	4,000-5,000
Range	8000-14,000
Range top, separate	4,000-8,000
Roaster	1,200-1,650
Rotisserie (broiler)	1,200-1,650
Toaster	500 - 900
Waste disposer	500 - 900

Food Storage

Freezer, household	300 - 500
Refrigerator	150 - 300
Refrigerator, frostless	400 - 600

Environmental Comfort

Air conditioner/central	2,500-5,000
Air conditioner/room	800 - 2,500
Blanket	150 - 200
Dehumidifier	250
Fan, portable	50 - 200
Heat lamp (infrared)	250
Heater, portable	1,000-1,500
Heater, wall-mounted	1,000-4,500
Heater, waterbed	800
Humidifier	450

Laundry

Appliance	Watts
Dryer	4,000-6,000
Iron, hand	600 - 1,200
Washing machine	300 - 350
Washing machine, automatic	500 - 800
Water heater	2,000-5,000

Personal Care

Hair dryer	350 - 1,200
Heating pad	50 - 75
Shaver	8 - 12

Entertainment

Projector, slide/movie	300 - 500
Radio (tube type)	40 - 150
Stereo (solid state)	30 - 100
TV, b/w (tube type)	150 - 325
TV, b/w (solid state)	50 - 100
TV, color (tube type)	300 - 450
TV, color (solid state)	150 - 250
VCR	40 - 70

Miscellaneous

Clock	2 - 3
Lamps, flourescent	15 - 60
Lamps, incandescent	10 upward
Sewing maching	60 - 90
Vacuum cleaner	250 - 1,200

Motors

¼ hp	300 - 400
½ hp	450 - 600
Over ½ hp/hp	950 - 1,000

120 volts x 30 amps=3600 watts   watts ÷ volts = amps

Batteries

Even the 12 vdc system (battery and converter) is dependent upon the 120 vac supplied by the shore power or generator to recharge the battery and to operate the 12 vdc system indefinitely. When the RV is running on the shore power cord (or the generator) many converters will recharge or help to maintain the charge for the coach or "house" battery. However, they can only partially recharge this battery. Most of the information we have received suggests that the converter will not fully charge a battery. Also, some rigs are wired to have the converter also help maintain the charge on the vehicle engine battery. The converter's main duty is to supply the 12 vdc required for the low-voltage lights, TV, stereo, vent fans, and furnace fan-motor. It also runs the electronic ignition modules for the furnace, refrigerator, and hot water heater, and the many other low-voltage devices.

The 12 vdc system also supplies the constant power required for the alarm systems such as the "gas-sniffer," a burglar or tamper alarm, and sometimes even the smoke detector. With all these systems depending upon the house battery for an energy source, a well-maintained battery and charging system is essential. As mentioned before, the converter is the normal method for keeping the house-battery partially charged; however, it is also possible and even recommended that you use other means and methods. Thus, we will mention a few of them that may prove to be worthwhile, according to the way you live your roaming life:

Portable Battery Chargers

These are the small chargers that many hardware stores and auto discount outlets sell to the "shadetree mechanic," which Gene claims to be. They are handy little devices that have an output of 1 to 10 amps of charging current. They will "taper-down" the charging rate as the battery becomes fully-charged. With one of these units attached to your battery whenever you are connected to shore power, or your generator is running, it is possible to keep the house-battery fully charged—a prerequisite, especially for boondocking. These chargers are relatively inexpensive and can be a real boon when you find that your car battery or tow vehicle battery is low.

Safety. Whenever you are dealing with a storage battery and a charger, it is wise to follow all the safety instructions published and shipped with the device. When working with or around a storage (lead-acid) battery, you must observe at least these four precautions:

1. Be careful not to get any of the electrolyte on your hands, clothing or any of the surrounding surfaces that can be damaged. This can cause severe burns on your skin and deterioration of your clothes.

2. If the battery has vent caps, remove them before charging. If there are no vent caps, be sure to follow the manufacturer's instructions as to rate of charge and where the charging is to take place. Charge only in a well-ventilated area.

3. Be very careful in connecting the charger. Observe the proper polarity when connecting the leads—generally, the RED lead goes to the POSITIVE (+) terminal, and the BLACK lead goes to the NEGATIVE (-) terminal.

4. No smoking, cooking, welding, or any other type of flames, sparks, or source of ignition should be near the charging battery. It gives off hydrogen gas as it is charging, which is extremely flammable.

Solar Charging Systems

A type of charging system now offered to RV travelers is the solar panel and charging system for the 12 vdc batteries used in your RV. Until recently, these devices were experimental and more of a fad. However, there are some quite substantial systems available at this time. Unless you plan to do extensive boondocking, though, their current high cost does not justify these systems for the average full-timer.

The solar charger system consists of a panel (or a group of

panels) that has several photo-electric cells placed on its surface. These are connected in series to provide a voltage of approximately 16-18 volts at a current rating of .5 to 3.5 amps, depending on the number and type of photo cells incorporated. This is then connected to the RV storage battery through a regulator and diode. When sunlight, or even a bright sky, falls on the panel and thus the cells, it produces a voltage and the system is arranged to recharge the battery.

The solar panels "store up" the sun's energy in a battery during the day, and thus make it available for use at night. Theoretically, as long as nighttime usage does not exceed the daily output of the solar panel, the charge is indefinitely maintained on the storage battery.

Safety. Because the solar panel is so closely associated to the 12 volt battery system, you must observe all of the safety requirements of that system. Keeping the panels clean, and watching your step around them to prevent breakage, are two of the more practical and immediate precautions for solar systems.

Environmental Control Devices

Staying Warm

There are many types of heating devices for the RV, and many types of fuels required for their operation. These are described in detail in Chapter 9. Other items to be considered for staying warm are the planning of proper clothing, adequate blankets (including electric blankets), and other bedcovers. Rain gear, coats, and boots are also of consideration when planning to stay warm and dry.

When traveling, full-timers get to experience all kinds of weather—sometimes all in one day! So it is advisable to be prepared. We try to plan our itinerary so that we are located where the weather suits our clothes. For the most part we stay where it is warm enough to wear summer clothing the year around. If you keep moving with the sun, you can keep your wardrobe fairly simple.

Staying Cool

It is impossible to predict the weather and sometimes we go too far south or stay too long in the desert, so the heat becomes uncomfortable. Again, we can turn to the ever-reliable electricity and turn on the air conditioner, the evaporative cooler, or the fans. Of course, to use the air conditioner, we must either be plugged into shore power or run our generator (you can find more details on these various means to comfort in Chapter 9).

Safety

Most of us are not accustomed to the heat of the deserts, the thin air in the mountains, or the cold conditions that can hit unexpectedly in any area in which we are traveling. And most of us will want to explore and visit as many places as we can. So off we go, in the summertime or even in the early fall, when the extremely high temperatures, combined with the low humidity of some of these places, will tend to catch even the natives unaware. They can present health risks to the uninitiated.

Because the humidity is so low, if the temperature is higher than we are accustomed to, we do not notice it so readily. When in extremely warm, hot, and dry climates, it is wise to watch how to dress and to be very cautious concerning the loss of body fluids.

When walking or hiking, be sure to take protective covering for your head and carry water with you into unfamiliar areas. Always keep a watchful eye upon your partner(s) and look for any of the following signs of heat exhaustion (formerly called "heatstroke" or "sunstroke"), an extremely dangerous condition:

- Pale face (or appearance of whitish splotches on the face);

- Dry, clammy skin on hands and arms;

- Fever and glazed look in the eyes;

- Any general loss of the ability to perspire;

- Shortness of breath (or any difficulty breathing);

- Weakness or the feeling of fainting or even nausea; or

- Any sense of disorientation.

If any of these symptoms occur, have someone immediately notify the police (or park rangers or other authorities) for help. Have the person sit, or better, lie out of the sun and take small sips of cool water. Try to bring the body temperature down with wet compresses on the forehead, and loosen all restrictive clothing. Be sure to obtain help as soon as possible. None of this information is intended to replace the advice of your doctor or physician, so contact one immediately.

Entertainment Devices

Television, VCR's

Television is probably the first device that any of us think of when the word entertainment is mentioned. Cable services now in our homes (and even more campgrounds across the country) allow access to movies, sporting events, and spectacular shows and news from around the world. VCR's tend to further enhance our dependence upon the TV set for entertainment.

We can watch movies whenever we are in the mood. Also, we can see movies made of our children, grandchildren, and other members of our family and friends in our own living room. And we can do this anywhere we are.

Radios

Broadcast, shortwave, ham, and CBs are all classes of radio service that the full-timer may find of use or of interest. We are all familiar with the standard broadcast bands for both AM and FM stations. Gene loves to listen to a good baseball or football game as we travel. Also, whenever we can, we tune into a radio drama as we journey. Some stations still have "The Green Hornet," "Inner Sanctum," or any of several new story lines. These and the many call-in talk shows are great ways to enjoy the driving hours. Generally, you can receive radio stations much more readily at a remote campsite than television signals.

We've also found a wonderful Public Library service—the ability to check out old radio show audio tapes. If you're just going to be away from an area for a few weeks, it's fun to listen to these programs as you travel.

Shortwave and ham radio are also very compatible with the full-time RV life. There are many RV clubs that use their equipment and service during rallies and emergencies.

The CB radio, which has been almost completely taken over by the truckers on Channel 19, is a source of entertainment and valuable information. By monitoring this channel, often you will learn of road blocks, accidents, or highway damage in the immediate vicinity. Early in our travels, we found that the CB radio was a most valuable device to have:

This is the story that we referred to in Chapter 10, when we awoke to find our batteries were too low to start the engine. We had purchased a small (50cc) motor scooter as supplemental transportation, and had fabricated a carrier rack on the back bumper of the S-10 pickup to carry it.

When we unhooked the truck to use its battery for jump-starting the motorhome, we also had to loosen the restraining straps for the scooter to get the jumper cables out of the back of the truck. After Gene started the motorhome and connected the truck back on its hitch, he decided to stow the jumper cables behind the seat in the truck, and so forgot to secure the scooter.

After pulling out onto the highway and attaining cruising speed, we heard a frantic call over the CB to the "east-bound motorhome": "You're losing your motorscooter!"

Our scooter had dropped down and was dragging along the

highway. To think that it might have eventually broken free and gone through someone's windshield is cause for severe emotional stress. But the CB and the thoughtfulness of that trucker thankfully averted a disaster. As embarrassing as this story is, we tell it to illustrate the utility of the CB channels.

Another valuable use of the CB is the voice contact we have between the person in the motorhome and the driver of our transportation vehicle. When we make short haul campground changes, it is sometimes easier for Deanne to drive the truck instead of towing it. We can expedite entry into the next campground without getting in and out of the motorhome. Also, we can drive the truck into the campground to locate a good campsite. We have found that using the CB to communicate during this separation is immensely helpful. It saves getting the motorhome into places where maneuvering is difficult.

Tape/CD Players

The use of music and learning cassette tapes is widespread, and the time spent traveling affords many opportunities for these pursuits. Music tapes are rapidly being replaced by the portable or mobile compact disc (CD) player. There is music available in this format for every taste, by almost every artist.

Where to Store Everything

Pods and Compartments

Extra clothes, bedding, seasonal articles, tools, and sundry items for living on the road will need to have their place if they are to accompany you. It is up to you to determine the use of each of your storage compartments and to assign every article a place to be kept when not in use. These articles can be items like table fans and portable electric heaters or electric blankets, coats or boots—articles needed only during a specific time.

We added a topside pod to carry the seasonal clothes that we must take with us, because of the work we do as we travel.

You will want to store kitchen articles such as electric skillets, blenders, can openers, popcorn poppers, and many other types of appliances or cookware until they are needed. We can only recommend that you weigh the necessity of each item that you take with you. Find items that can serve multiple purposes if you can. For instance, we use pizza pans for cookie sheets, and our electric skillet also serves as a griddle for hot cakes.

Tools

Tools are a real necessity for the many projects in your RV, or for helping others whenever they need it. You may only want to take the tools that will enable you to take care of an emergency such as a leaky faucet or other small task. Whatever your skills or hobbies, you will want to be equipped for them.

Files and a Safe

A place for your necessary personal papers is also important. We have several files that we carry with us. Some suggestions for these papers are the new style milk crates—those large, heavy plastic containers with the correct dimensions to hang the Pendaflex Files within them. You can buy them in a local department store such as K-Mart or Wal Mart. Some even have lids so you can stack them and keep the files inside clean. We find these boxes fit nicely under our galley table seats. If your papers are not so extensive, you may want to find a simple file folder or file box.

The use of a fire-proof safe may also be something that you want to consider. It can be permanently installed within closets, or under floors that extend into an outside compartment.

Weight Limits

After deciding what you want to take with you and placing all of it in its proper place, be sure that you have not violated your rig's weight limits. These limits are stated in the manufacturer's documents that you received with the purchase of your rig. They are also shown somewhere on the title plate for the unit.

If this limit is exceeded, you run the risk of violating any warranty on your RV. Also, many problems may appear in the operation of your rig. You may get poor service from your tires, or cracks may develop in the frame or other vital areas of your RV. Extreme violations may lead to dangerous handling conditions with wheel and axle breakage a possibility. You may be forced to leave some of your "necessities" behind.

Rental Storage

Rental storage is an option for any leftover items that you can't take with you. Check your area Yellow Pages under "Storage" for the availability of these storage units. Another option is to rent space in a friend or relative's garage, attic, or basement.

Take only what you need. Save what you think you may decide you need later. When you've pared it down to what you can or need to carry, have a garage sale of your stored items again. If you haven't used it in a few years, you probably won't use it at all. Don't get tied to your possessions.

We purchased an RV so we could move, yet sometimes we find that we've loaded it with so many things, it's easier to leave the RV where it is and drive our truck where we need to go. This defeats our purpose, and it's at these revelations that we decide it's time to pare down again.

Section III:

Go!

14

BUT CAN THIS RV BE MADE INTO OUR HOME?

"Except the Lord build the house,
they labour in vain that build it . . ."
Psalm 127:1

In our travels, we have met people who are seemingly so in awe of their RV and the manufacturer's decor, that they live in it just as it came from the factory. Thus, they dwell in an environment which lacks in the expression of their individual personalities and tastes.

We decided long ago that if our RV was to be our home, we should decorate it and rearrange the furniture to suit our style of living. There was no reason to live in our stationary home with unsightly warning signs and other dealer or manufacturer's labels in full view (on window panes, inside or outside of cupboards, and on appliances). Thus, it was not desirable that these remain in our RV home. As an example, most manufacturers place seat belt warning labels on the walls near each seat or chair in the RV.

Once we became the owners of our RV and were aware of all the warnings and labels, it was not necessary for these to be in full view. Thus, we removed the labels and placed any needed information in a file for each item.

We hung pictures on the walls, decorated, and arranged the furniture to suit us. As we put each item in place, we found that we had to make a choice concerning it: Was the item to remain in a permanently assigned place, or did we plan for it to move about within our home? We didn't plan to move pictures and knickknacks, so placed them in a fixed location. Books, magazines, coasters, and other like items would be used in different locations, so they couldn't be fixed in place.

We used several methods for anchoring the fixed-location items to prevent them from falling or swinging about as we traveled. Then, we established a list of items that we decided to pack carefully whenever we traveled (see Chapter 16, Checklists). This chapter will discuss several of these methods and give you ideas for your own RV.

Customizing the Living Space

New Cabinets

Before we moved into our RV as a permanent home, we determined that we would need additional cabinet space in the bathroom and the galley.

In the Bathroom

The bathrooms in most RVs are functional, but tend to be spartan when it comes to storage. We surveyed the options and determined that the wall area directly over and behind the commode would provide a convenient space for an additional cabinet. We purchased the cabinet from our local Sears Outlet Store at a close-out price. It matches the rest of the cabinetry so well that no one would guess that it was added.

In the Galley

Deanne wanted to take a set of china and crystal glassware along with us in the motorhome for the times we entertained—or at least did not want to use paper plates and cups for our meals.

This required some consideration about how and where to properly increase our space to fit their storage.

In our particular floorplan, we found that the space over the galley sink provided an ideal site to install a new cabinet. We decided the area was the right size to hold a standard kitchen cabinet (the type that is normally placed over the refrigerator in a stationary home).

Gene drilled and fastened the cabinet to the ceiling and butted it into the existing cabinet. In our motorhome, there is also a two-inch steel roll-bar, to which we could fasten the back of the cabinet.

The front, sides, and bottom of this cabinet were prefinished, but the back was not. Thus, we finished it in a way that was decorative, inexpensive, and useful. The bottom of the cabinet was inset upward approximately one inch. This would provide an open area in which we could run wiring for an undercabinet light fixture, once we installed a wide, prefinished shelf-board to its underside.

Another kitchen cabinet gave us room for even more dishes.

Because this shelf-board (now the cabinet bottom) was approximately three inches wider (front to back) than the cabinet, the addition of some ship's railing created a knickknack shelf. By attaching a mirror to the back of the cabinet, we finished it nicely. It then became a place to keep some little things that make a house a home, beyond its serviceability as an extra cupboard.

The knickknacks displayed on this shelf are all semi-permanently fastened down with a substance called dollhouse wax. You can purchase this wax wherever dollhouse furniture and supplies are sold. It is very sticky and fairly strong, and a dab or two will hold most any item of this type quite well. You can experiment with the placement of the items, as the wax can be removed easily from your furniture or knickknacks.

This cabinet and shelf tend to present an obstacle to tall visitors (and those who move fast without watching) in our home. It can cause a bump on the head if they don't watch out. Thus, to call attention to its presence and provide more additional storage, Gene hung a stemware rack on the underside of the cabinet. It doesn't always prevent bumps, but it helps.

The back of the cabinet gave us a knick-knack shelf.

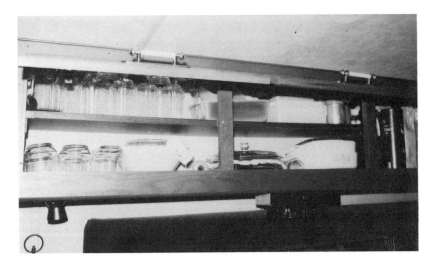

Adding these shelves doubled our usuable space.

Divider Shelves in Overhead Cabinets

The original shelf space in our overhead galley cabinets was inadequate for—and extravagant of—the storage space for cups and glasses. These cabinets were tall inside, and left half the enclosed space unused where short glasses and cups were stored.

Gene took the inside measurements of the cabinet and purchased a prefinished shelf of the proper dimensions from the local home goods store. He cut off one end of the shelf at a point exactly behind the second door facing. The end of the shelf was supported by a cleat fastened to the end cabinet wall at the proper height. Gene used the cutoff piece as a support for the other end of the shelf, with enough length left over to make a stop for the shelf. This prevents items from sliding off the top of the shelf into the next cabinet area. This simple addition effectively doubled our shelf space in the overhead cabinet.

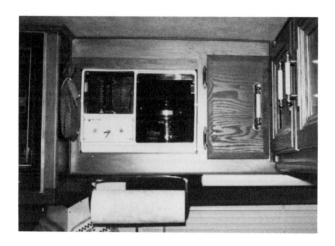

Our coffee maker fits perfectly in this overhead cabinet.

Coffee Maker

Our first week on the road paid dividends for us when we discovered we were parked in a campsite directly opposite a "twin sister" to our own motorhome. We were (and still are) so excited about our new life that we visited our new neighbors as soon as possible. We wanted to compare notes and see how they liked their twin home.

Upon entering, the first thing we noticed was their coffee maker. The cabinet next to the microwave had the door removed and now contained an under-the-counter coffee brewer. After some discussion and investigation, we found our own motorhome was pre-wired for this installation. Another space problem was solved.

Knife Block

When we moved into the motorhome, we brought our set of good knives in their storage block. Every time we moved the motorhome, we had to safely stow the knife block. We soon found a simple solution for anchoring it to the cabinet, without permanently fixing it in place:

Gene drilled two quarter-inch holes into the countertop (spaced approximately ten inches apart) and glued a dowel into each hole, leaving one inch of each protruding upward. Matching holes were then drilled into the underside of the knife block to hold it in place. The knife block has thus traveled thousands of miles with us and has never moved from its location, unless we lift it to clean underneath.

Cutting Board/Cover for Stove Top

In spite of all the good points we found in our RV, there were some drawbacks. One pitfall became apparent shortly after beginning our full-timing odyssey: the lack of cabinet-top working space.

Neither Deanne nor Gene is a gourmet cook, but we still need some work space to open those cans of beans and boxes of macaroni and cheese!

Cutting boards add needed counter space to an RV galley.

We discussed our dilemma with our brother-in-law. For Christmas that year he constructed a unique and practical oak cutting board that fits perfectly over the cooktop, greatly extending the preparation area for these amateur cooks. We use this board for cutting vegetables and meat, and move it to the table when preparing cookies and pies. It is designed to travel in place over the cooktop and is only removed for cooking or baking. When the stove burners are on, we turn the cutting board sideways and it slips conveniently between the stovetop and the wall.

AC Lighting and Swing Lamps

As we discussed before, these incandescent lights tend to make your rig feel like home due to the warmth (or feeling of warmth) they provide. We prefer them for reading lights and for any close-up work.

Sometimes you can mount a table top lamp on the small table between the swivel chairs in the living room. Most motorhomes have inadequate end tables for permanently mounting table lamps near the sofa or gaucho. We found that the best place to install these lights is on a wall near your favorite reading area. Be sure there is a nearby AC outlet wherever your place your lamps, so you won't be running extension cords in dangerous places.

Hollow-Core Door Fasteners

Whenever we need to permanently mount something to the walls or ceiling of our rig, we have found that the "molly-bolt" type of fastener, designed for hollow-core doors, works great. This fastener will close down to the thickness of the plywood veneer used in the walls of most RVs. We have employed them to fasten our swing arm lamps to the walls near our reading areas; to repair the closet rods that have pulled down from the ceiling; and to mount our telephones to the walls. They were used to install our ceiling fan over the bed (just don't stand in the middle of the bed—our tallest daughter claims she has bald spots in the shape of fan blades), and many other projects.

Desk

A major change we made in our RV, to create our home, was the removal of the factory swivel chairs and the folding table group. In their place we installed a roll-top desk with a computer and printer. We fully intended to replace a swivel chair with an RV chair. However, we were so discouraged by the cost that we bought a standard swivel rocker from a furniture store for a very reasonable price. Add the word "RV" to any normal item, and the price triples, while the value may be the same, but never better. We use a typist chair at the desk, and thus have a comfortable place to handle our business.

The knee-hole in our desk provided a handy place to build more shelves in the back half of it. Paper supplies, the printer (while traveling), and other office provisions fit snugly in this area, and are out of the way (yet easy to reach while working).

Gene fabricated dowels from quarter-inch brass welding rods that keep the desk drawers from opening when we are enroute. He drilled the top of the desk directly over each drawer front, and put a matching hole in the top of the drawer. The dowel slides down nicely as a lock. Quarter-inch, brass eyelets (designed for fabric) were inserted and glued into each hole (desk top and drawer front edge) to prevent the wooden holes from enlarging. A bungie cord holds a chair in the knee-hole, and keeps the shelf items in place as we travel.

The desk lamp, computer monitor, and the copy holder are all permanently fastened to the desk top with screws. The desk is then fastened to the motorhome floor with standard metal corner wedges that are used in furniture construction. These are available at most hardware or building supply stores.

Gene constructed a unique shelf unit, which he calls a "printer bridge," that is placed between the front seats, and is supported by the armrests. This bridge supports the printer, its paper supply, and reference materials when we are set up in a campground.

Drop-Leaf Table

We originally thought we would have to get rid of the drop-leaf table that sat between the two swivel chairs. We found that, although it took up some space, putting it between the passenger and driver chairs, facing backward, made a wonderfully handy coffee table in front of the couch. We let it down when not in use, and raise it to double as a coffee table or an extra table in front of the desk when needed for large projects. The table is fastened to the rear of the engine cover with two strong slide bolts. It thus can be moved when necessary to work on the engine or unfold the sofa into a bed.

Dowel rods allow easy closing of privacy curtains.

Front Curtain Push/Pull Rods

With the printer bridge in place, the front privacy curtains were difficult to close or open. There was no way to get to the tracks to pull or push the curtains. We inserted a dowel rod into the leading hem of each curtain (retaining them in place with a couple of staples at the end). They then became easy to open or close just by grasping the bottom of the dowel and pulling or pushing the curtain into place.

Awning Rod Storage

Most of the awnings installed on an RV come with a removable arm or a rod. This pulls the awning down from the middle, allowing one person to use or operate levers or controls located on the awning assembly. We failed to include this rod in our checklist of things to stow and, much to our chagrin, left it behind in some distant campground.

Prior to this experience, we stored this long, awkward item under the front edge of the sofa. Here it was out of the way and sadly, also out of sight. After its subsequent loss, Gene made a new rod out of a four-foot piece of "all-thread" rod. We installed a pair of small-tool clips near the entry door. The rod is snapped into the clips, and is thus stored flush to the wall vertically and unobtrusively. It can be retrieved from outside when necessary, or checked to make sure it is with us by just a glance.

TV/VCR Center

When we purchased our RV, it had a beautiful bar console with a lighted, mirrored, glass and bottle display rack installed on top of a cabinet over a built-in ice maker. While the rack was eye-pleasing and decorative, we could find no practical use for it other than that for which it was designed. Also, a small, nine-inch color television was built into a cabinet directly over the bar, and the TV proved woefully small for viewing from the living room.

We removed the bar console and the television from the upper cabinet. The cupboard door from the cabinet where the coffee maker had been positioned fit perfectly. We installed it over the front of the TV cabinet, thus creating a new cupboard. We just use the nine-inch TV for shadetree baseball games, and bought a replacement 19-inch TV with a built-in VCR. Now we have a complete and adequate sized video entertainment center, which is easily seen from the living room and is equally as decorative as the bar. We find the ice maker a wonderful appliance in our home—how did we ever do without one?

Table With Condiment Shelf

Our coach came equipped with a dinette that was touted as a supplemental bed. However, it could not be used by an adult or child over the age of ten. The table top, which was also to serve as the center section of the bed, was only twenty-two inches wide. It was not wide enough to hold more than two plates, and those could not be placed directly opposite each other. Remember, most RVs are not designed for full-time living, and while this table might have been all right for camping, it was not suitable for every meal. But these are all shortcomings that can only be ferreted out by the living-in-it experience.

Knowing that we never intended to use the dinette as a bed, we decided to do something about this inadequate eating space. At a garage sale, we discovered a table top that was left over from a restaurant remodeling operation. It has a formica oak-grain top and was the perfect width for our use. We purchased the entire table top for $5.00 and it required only a single saw-cut to make it fit.

Dinette table with matching condiment shelf.

Gene cut one end to butt it up to the wall. He then removed the leg and wall hardware from the old table top and attached it to the new one. The cut-off end was attached to some short legs and now sits under the window. This provides a convenient shelf for a planter, books, and condiments. Rubber feet on the bottom of the legs allow the shelf to remain in place as we travel.

Built-In Vacuum Cleaner

One feature of our motorhome at the time of purchase was a built-in vacuum cleaner. The manufacturer of our motorhome had placed this unit in a compartment under a dinette seat, with the hose connection located under the dinette, between the two seats. This location required getting down on our hands and knees to connect the hose to it.

A door was installed for access into the compartment but the arrangement of the vacuum cleaner under the seat made it impossible to store the accessories or the hose through the door. This door also could not be used to change the vacuum cleaner bag. The only way to store the accessories and hose—and to service the unit—was to remove the seat cushions and raise the loose board that covered the compartment.

It only made sense to move the whole vacuum cleaner to a more useful location. This would not only make it more convenient, but would also free up the compartment under the seat for use as a file storage area.

Directly beneath the seat storage area was an outside compartment of the proper dimensions to allow installation of the cleaning unit. This arrangement not only moved the noise to the outside, but it also meant the dirt and dust of changing the bag was also outdoors. Also, this installation made it simple to run PVC pipe under the motorhome to the rear and to the front, thus allowing for two hose outlets in more convenient locations.

A place for shoes when not under foot.

Shoe Storage

The nature of our work, and the resulting requirement for dress clothes and dress shoes, and casual shoes for everyday, created storage problems. A partial solution was found when we purchased an over-the-door, pocket shoe storage unit.

By cutting the unit lengthwise, two pockets fit perfectly inside each of two closet doors. Thus, six pairs of shoes were stored out of sight. We store additional shoes on the floor of the shirt closets on either side of the bed.

Gene also found an area under the bed, next to the fresh water storage tank, which was unused. This area was approximately thirteen inches wide, about forty inches long, and fifteen inches high. Gene cut an opening in the side of the bed frame and installed a door. He then placed a wire shelf inside to divide the area, and Deanne now has storage space for fifteen to twenty pairs of high heels.

Installing a Safe

We strongly recommend that everyone who intends to live in their RV install a good fire-proof safe. Keep everything that is irreplaceable in the safe (insurance papers, copies of your will, passport, ownership papers, negotiable stocks or bonds, cash, and jewelry). Have the safe installed in a way that precludes having it easily removed. Bolt it down to floor, have it welded to the frame of the RV, or hide it under false fronts. A larger, built-in safe with a less secure locking system may prove to be more secure than a smaller (easily carried) one with highly secure locks. A thief may not take the time to pick the lock if he can just walk off with the safe. He can thus be in and out of your RV quicker than anyone can catch him.

Protection from loss by fire is probably a more critical reason for having a safe than theft, when you consider how quickly an RV can burn. Keep your valuables in the fireproof safe and always pre-plan your own escape routes.

Decorative Items Hung on the Walls

Pictures, plaques, and clocks can be attached to the walls of your RV in several ways. Foam, double-sided tape will hold most items in place. If you plan to hang pictures of the family (ones that are renewed from time to time), attach the frames to the wall with a hook and loop material like Velcro™.

Note

Velcro™ is magic stuff. We put it on the bottom facing of our wallmounted telephone so the receiver cannot come off the hook inadvertently. It works great.

Drill the frames of heavier pictures and fasten them in place with screws or hollow-core door fasteners.

Fold-Down Shelves

After living in our RV for only a short while, we discovered shortcomings in the way of shelf space. Unless one was sitting at the dinette table, there was no place to set down a cup of coffee or cold drink while reading or watching television. Also, when we went to sleep, there was no night stand at the side of the bed for a clock, pair of glasses, or the book or magazine we were reading. Our bedroom wall also had a large, beautiful mirror at the foot of the bed, but no place to set make-up items or a comb and brush, which would allow more than one person to dress at a time.

To overcome the initial problem of no shelves, Gene again went to the hardware store and obtained some prefinished oak shelves, brackets, and piano hinges. He fastened these to the walls at desired locations and supported them with the brackets while in the down position. When these shelves are not needed they can be lifted up and stored out of the way, against the wall.

Gene bought a make-up light bar for placing lights over the mirror in the bedroom, and this shelf became a make-up center for Deanne.

Throw Rugs

As we mentioned earlier in the book, a few throw rugs in selected places protect the carpeting and personalize your coach. After traveling a few miles in your RV with throw rugs down, though, you will find that they seem to have legs of their own. They tend to "walk" forward in the coach and are always out-of-place. The biggest problem is not that they are not where you want them, but the danger they cause should a person trip over them when they bunch up.

We have heard of several methods for fastening these rugs down and keeping them in place. Some people use carpet tacks and tack them where they want them. Others have tried velcro, and some use double-sided tape to tape them in place. Some ambitious folks have even resorted to the needle and thread method, and *sewn* them in place.

Our solution has been to snap these rugs down to the floor with do-it-yourself snaps. The female snap portion is placed on each corner of the rug, and its matching male portion is screwed to the floor at the desired location for the throw rug. The throw rug remains in place while we travel, and we need only unsnap them for cleaning the carpet underneath or shaking the rugs.

Summer Heat Protection

As we mentioned in Chapter 11, the inside of your RV is subject to extremely high temperatures. This is especially true in the summer, or in the south where the sun is out for long periods of the day. Ventilation is the first line remedy to control this high interior heat build-up.

Ceiling vents can be left open to allow the heat to escape through natural convection. When these vents are closed you can feel the heat build up near them, and some of that heat is from the sun beating down through the vent cover itself.

For about $14.00, camping supply stores sell an insulated vinyl covering for these vents to stop that heat build-up (they also insulate and prevent heat loss in the winter). However, you can't open the vent and let heat out with this covering in place.

Thus, we recommend the installation of automotive shades (those designed for preventing glare into your car without blocking your view). This substitute still allows the vent to operate. These shades sell for anywhere from $3.00 to $7.00 each, and are the perfect size for covering a vent. They are usually black on one side, and white (or some other lighter color) on the other, to reflect the heat back out. They are perforated with thousands of tiny holes that let you see through them, thus allowing air to pass through. We have installed these on each of our ceiling vents and they have drastically reduced the interior heat build-up within the motorhome during summer sunshine.

We have also installed a small, thirty-six inch ceiling fan over the center of our bed, to circulate the air and prevent heat build-up in the bedroom. This is cheaper and quieter than the air conditioner and can run virtually day and night in the summer-time.

Another efficient and passive method is simply to tint the windows. Check with your state's authorities to learn if you can tint the windows in the driver-passenger area of a motorhome. One side benefit to tinted windows is the protection of your furniture and drapery material from sun fading. Another benefit is enhanced privacy, as most tinting prevents viewing the inside of your home from outside (not at night with the lights on inside, though. Watch out!).

Customizing the Driver-Passenger Area

Dash instruments such as tachometers, temperature gauges for transmission and engine oil, electronic compasses, indoor-outdoor electronic thermometers, inclinometer, altimeters, CB radios, and rear-view TV systems are all available to make the driver's job easier and much more efficient. When you discover a need, we are confident that you can find a solution to it.

A trip to any camping or RV supply store will convince you that whatever you may need or desire is available to enhance your comfort as a passenger or driver. There are beaded seat covers, air-conditioned seat covers, window shades, visor extenders, beverage holders, beverage dispensers, fans, heaters, back and/or tush supporters, reading lights, snooze pillows, and comforters, to name a few.

Customizing the Outside of the RV

Ground Tank/Auxiliary LP Tank

In Chapter 13 we discussed the necessity for this addition to a motorhome. It has proven itself repeatedly as we have used it crossing the country.

Satellite TV Antenna

This is an accessory most people will consider a luxury. However, if you plan to spend much of your time as a boondocker, or camping in remote sections of the country, it can be a necessity. The use of a satellite antenna will allow you to watch news from around the country, and bring in many entertainment opportunities. Mainly, it will allow you to make choices about how isolated and cut off from the rest of the world you want to be.

Standard VHF-UHF TV Antenna

Today you will have to look hard to find an RV (other than a pickup camper or tent trailer) that doesn't have some sort of provision for television reception. There are many manufacturers of TV antennas; some are good and some are better. If you decide that you need one, look around in your local campground and ask people what they're using and see how they work. If you look at several operations you can make a better choice based on experience.

Satellite antennas can catch the news from afar.

Pods

A rooftop pod for additional storage is, to our way of thinking, a compromise solution. They are expensive, but not as expensive as replacing your present RV with a basement model. You will also be trading off a small percentage of fuel usage due to the increased wind resistance. Still, it is cheaper than trading before you are ready. Also, it is easier to add a pod than to try to convince yourself that it is time to trim down your possessions.

There are several manufacturers of pods and storage compartments for RV use. We cannot recommend the relatively inexpensive "cartop" carriers as full-time storage units. The material from which they are constructed cannot stand up to continuous exposure to sunlight.

Pods that are manufactured for RV use are constructed of heavier gauge material and have internal metal frames for strength and security. This frame also makes it possible to create a better weather seal than can be found on the cheaper units. Basically, you will get what you pay for.

Another approach is to decide how much you want to spend on the pod, based on what will be stored in it. How secure must it be? If you plan to store expensive clothing and luggage in it, you would be well advised to buy the best. How weather-resistant must it be? If you plan to store items that can take weather or dust and dirt, and have value only in your eyes, use the cartop carrier and replace it as necessary. These units cost 75-80% less than RV pods of the same relative size. However, they will only stand up to two or three seasons before beginning to deteriorate from the sun.

Gene asks, "Why don't they make pods and air conditioner covers out of the same material as those plastic grocery bags that never degrade? The covers only last about four years on top of an RV before they turn to powder when you touch them."

There has been some improvement in this area. Camping World sells replacement covers for air conditioners that are fabricated from sheet metal. Check with them or your local RV parts supplier for more information.

15

WHAT ARE SOME TIPS FOR MAINTAINING OUR RV INSIDE AND OUT?

"Be thou diligent to know the state of thy flocks, and look well to thy herds."
Proverbs 27:23

Deanne feels that the best thing about not having a large home is not having to clean it. Whereas she always cleaned house a little at a time, we each now take a half of our entire home and we're done with major cleaning in an hour or so.

Once, when we were lamenting the fact that we never had to wash the outside of our stationary home, we remembered that we did have to keep it painted. It helped, as we used that elbow grease to wash and wax our RV.

One night we thought we could save on the noise and confinement of having to run the air conditioner by parking our motorhome under some beautiful pine trees for shade. It was pleasant, smelled good, and was relaxing to hear the pine needles falling on our rooftop. The next day, to our great chagrin, we discovered that those pine needles dripped pine sap as they lay drying on our rooftop. What a mess! More washing and waxing—and another lesson learned.

We find that tire guards keep tires from rotting, and turf site rugs (and shoes removed) keep outside dirt out. Nylon RV covers (used when the RV is in storage whenever we leave for long periods of time) also lengthen the life of our RV home.

An innovative trick for keeping the front-end of our truck free from road tar, broken headlights, and a damaged windshield was the addition of a homemade mud flap across the rear of the motorhome. Although you can buy a broom-like unit from RV supply stores, Gene used a conveyor belt that was given to him. He cut it to length to fit just in front of the rear bumper, and bolted it to the frame of the motorhome. It works wonderfully, and although we were told it might adversely affect our gas mileage, we found that it actually improved it. The only thing Gene can attribute that to, is it probably decreased the air turbulence between the truck and the motorhome.

Our homemade mud guard

Housecleaning Tools

Although we find that our RV gets dustier than our stationary home did, we still came out ahead timewise on our routine cleaning. Here are some handy tools for saving time:

Vacuum Cleaner Versus Elbow Grease

When we discovered that we were getting a built-in vacuum in our new RV, Deanne's first inclination was to sell the little carpet sweeper we had used in our camping days. It was a good decision not to have sold that, the hand-held Dustbuster, or the broom. Daily cleaning goes much faster with such quickly-accessed tools.

Common Household Cleaners Without the "RV" Label

Murphy's Oil Soap is handy for cleaning cabinet fronts, table and desk tops, and the vinyl on the dashboard. One-Step floor polish not only works on our kitchen floor, but a thin layer applied to shower walls every six weeks keeps hard-water stains from forming. Our favorite cleaning tools are denture cleanser tablets. Put one in your drained toilet holding tank while you drive (with about an inch of clean water left in the tank). It sloshes around with the movement of the RV, removes hard-water build-up, and leaves the tank fresh-smelling. We think, quite honestly, that we feel better putting the tablets in the tank—rather than the tank receiving such marvelous benefits.

Note

> *In "emergency" situations, Pine-Sol and Clorox can be used in holding tanks as a deodorant/disinfectant (in lieu of the brand-name "blue stuff" you find in the RV supply stores). Be frugal, though, and don't make it an every-day practice. Clorox may harden the rubber seals on the dump valve.*

Keeping Those Tanks "Sparkling" Clean

Besides using holding tank deodorizer/cleaner in our toilets, Gene also installed a jet stream spray head in both the gray and black water holding tanks. This allows us to flush the tanks out internally with a garden hose whenever we dump. These really help in keeping solids from building up on the walls and floors of the tanks.

Maintenance Tips For Appliances

Waterproofing Circuit Boards

One of the first items to fail in our motorhome was the hot water heater. It would heat the water the first time, but would fail to re-ignite when the water was used. This required a complete restart before we could get hot water again.

Upon notifying Norcold, the manufacturer, we received (within three days) a replacement circuit board. They recommended that before we placed it in service, we coat it with shellack or some other waterproof coating. Their service department believed that the higher humidities in coastal regions could have an effect on the operation of this board. Since Gene worked in electronics, and was required to use waterproof conformal coating materials, it was no problem for him to obtain this product. He suggests that you contact an electronic contractor for information or a supply of the coating.

After receiving this advice, we discovered the same type of circuit boards are used in the refrigerator and both furnaces. We decided to use the coating on these boards as well. To date we have experienced no further problems with circuit boards.

Furnace Thermostat

After some time you may find that when you turn your furnace on and set the thermostat, the fan will blow, but the burner will not ignite. Gene has discovered that in checking the contacts on the thermostat, you may find them dark and pitted. If you clean them with a piece of emery paper (to make them bright and shiny) you may find that the furnace will then work properly. This problem may be due to high resistance in the contacts, which prevents the board from firing. It is worth checking to make sure before contacting a furnace man at high RV appliance service prices.

Handling Pests

We have never had any of the pests that sometimes show up in stationary homes, such as earwigs, cockroaches, mice and crickets. However, Brandy was good at bringing home special guests such as fleas and ticks. Once we parked on a fire-anthill in Alabama and had ants for weeks. Antrol cans, strategically placed, finally won out.

Spiders also show up periodically. We have gotten into the habit of taking a day away from the motorhome every six months and setting off two pest bombs to rid ourselves of anything that might be here, or thinking of coming in. What is our clue that it's time to bomb? Just like at home: bites.

Logbooks and Diaries

It's a nuisance, but for tax purposes (one benefit of working on the road: writing off your expenses) Deanne has kept a diary every day since we left "home." It has come in handy often and contains such information as: Where we've been and when we've been there; how many miles we drove; the rating of the campground so we know if we should return or not; and what we did when we were in a certain place.

These logbooks can be purchased in RV supply stores—or using a simple steno notebook will do.

Records of Maintenance

Records of oil changes, brake maintenance, tune-ups, tire rotations, and inspection of nuts and bolts (especially on tow bars and hitches) are also logged in our diary—and have been well worth the trouble of keeping track more than once.

If you take care of the small things, the big things will take care of themselves. Being on a tight budget, we have no choice. We feel that being good stewards of our money means taking care of what we have as conscientiously as possible. So we guess that even if it weren't necessary, we would still keep a diary/logbook.

16

How Will We Remember To Do Everything? (With Sample Checklists)

"Where there is no vision, the people perish;
but he that keepeth the law, happy is he."
Proverbs 29:18

Inside/Outside Checklists for
Moving, Setting Up and Storing our RV

Checklists may seem a waste of time, and a nuisance to continually update as you buy new, or discard old things in your coach. However, we have learned the hard way that a checklist to use before you travel, when you set up, and when you store your rig, is invaluable.

Not only did we have the experience with an unlocked refrigerator, but we also broke the step on our first motorhome when we failed to make sure it was up before driving through a toll booth in Oklahoma.

We drove off with our TV antenna extended once, until a nice man drove up beside us and told us of our situation. This caused us to watch for others who might have forgotten the same thing. Gene once walked over to a man who was filling his tank at a gas station to tell him his antenna was up. He was surprised when the man declared it was all right to travel with it extended. Gene apologized for butting in, but then heard the man say to his wife, "Betty, I told you to put that antenna down! We could have broken it off!"

We've included, as follows, a copy of our checklists for you to use as samples. Use them to make your own, individual ones. Then check that list *every time* you move or park or store your rig. It will save you a lot of money, inconvenience and frustration.

Motorhome—Travel—Checklist
(Outside Coach)

☐ Fill both holding tanks (gray and black) if water is available. Then . . .

☐ Drain as follows, at dump station or sewer hookup:
a. Black water tank first.
b. Then gray water, in order to flush hose.

☐ Disconnect sewer hose, wash with fresh water, stow.

☐ Install drain cap.

☐ Disconnect water hose (if used), drain and stow.

☐ Disconnect shore power (if used) and stow.

☐ Clean, retract, and secure awnings (if extended). Store handle inside coach on wall.

☐ Raise jacks and stow any leveling boards used.

☐ Remove "Townsend" sign and stow.

☐ Take down satellite antenna and stow.

☐ Secure and lock all outside hatches and rooftop pod.

(Outside of Coach When Towing Truck)

☐ Pack all ground equipment and tools in rear of truck.

☐ Install "Vehicle In Tow" sign in rear window of truck.

☐ Load bicycles and secure with hold-down straps.

☐ Cover bicycles with tarp and secure.

☐ Install tow-bar and connect truck to motorhome:
a. Connect light cord.
b. Connect safety cables
c. Check that lights on truck function with motorhome lights.

☐ Place truck transmission in neutral.

☐ Release truck parking brake.

☐ Using single ignition key, place ignition switch in "unlocked" position (the steering wheel will be free turning and the ignition "off"); leave key in switch.

☐ Turn wheels to straight position.

☐ Install windshield cover and lock truck doors.

(Inside Coach)

☐ Park the hard drive on the computer.

☐ Put bungie cord on desk chair. Secure desk drawers with pins.

☐ Turn burglar alarm off.

☐ Turn off front and rear furnace thermostats (if used).

☐ Turn off water heater.

☐ Switch refrigerator to "Gas" (or "Off" if necessary).

☐ Turn off icemaker (for prolonged trips).

☐ Lock refrigerator, freezer, and icemaker doors.

☐ Take soap dish and back scrubber off caddy, place in tub.

☐ Lower TV antenna and turn off red light.

☐ Turn on automatic step (verify that step retracts when door is closed).

☐ Secure and/or stow all loose articles inside coach, such as hanging plants, lampshades, knickknacks.

☐ Secure large TV.

☐ Take down bedroom fan.

☐ Put vents down.

☐ Shut and lock all windows.

☐ Snap bathroom shower curtain shut.

☐ Raise rear blind.

☐ Secure food under table.

☐ Snap front privacy curtains in place.

☐ Put bungie cord on closet door.

☐ Lock doors. Make sure step comes up.

Motorhome—Set-Up—Checklist
(Outside Coach)

☐ Disconnect truck from motorhome.

☐ Install any required leveling boards and extend jacks.

☐ Connect water hose (if available).

☐ Connect shore power (if available).

☐ Connect sewer hose (if available). Stow drain cap safely.

☐ Extend awnings. Store handle inside coach on wall (Use wind strap if required).

☐ Unlock outside hatches and rooftop pod to remove needed articles.

☐ Install "Townsend" sign.

☐ Set up satellite antenna.

(Inside Coach)

☐ Turn burglar alarm on (as required).

☐ Turn on front and rear furnace thermostats (if used).

☐ Turn on hot water heater (see noue under LP Gas—use of).

☐ Switch refrigerator to "Gas" (or "Electric" if available).

☐ Turn on icemaker.

☐ Unlock refrigerator, freezer, and icemaker doors. Check for spilled articles. Relock.

☐ Raise TV antenna and turn on red light.

☐ Turn off automatic step after it is extended.

☐ Set up all packed items, and loose articles inside coach, such as:
  a. Hanging plants.
  b. Lampshades.
  c. Statue on knickknack shelf.

☐ Remove bungie cord on desk chair. Remove pins from desk drawers.

☐ Put vents up (if desired).

☐ Unlock and open windows as desired.

☐ Lower rear blind.

☐ Install bedroom fan.

☐ Remove bungie cord from closet door. Store cord in closet.

Motorhome—Storage—Checklist
(Outside Coach)

☐ Fill both holding tanks (gray and black) if water is available. Then . . .

☐ Drain as follows, at dump station or sewer hookup:
a. Black water tank first.
b. Then gray water, in order to flush hose.

☐ Disconnect sewer hose (if used). Wash hose with fresh water, stow.

☐ Install drain cap.

☐ Place approximately one inch of water in each holding tank (see Inside Coach).

☐ Disconnect water hose (if used), drain and stow.

☐ Disconnect shore power (if used) and stow.

☐ Clean, retract, and secure awnings (if extended). Store handle inside coach on wall.

☐ Remove "Townsend" sign and stow.

☐ Take down satellite antenna and stow.

☐ Secure and lock all outside hatches and rooftop pod.

☐ Install outside coach cover and secure tightly.

(Inside Coach)

☐ Park the hard drive on the computer.

☐ Put bungie cord on desk chair. Secure desk drawers with pins.

☐ Put one inch of water in tanks, and add approximately four ounces of toilet chemical to each tank (see Outside Coach).

☐ Turn off front and rear furnace thermostats (if used).

☐ Turn off hot water heater.

☐ Switch refrigerator to "Off".

☐ Turn off icemaker.

☐ Remove contents, thoroughly clean inside and prop open refrigerator, freezer, and icemaker doors one inch.

☐ Remove all perishable foods from cupboards (for long-term storage).

☐ Lower TV antenna and turn off red light.

☐ Turn on automatic step, verify that step retracts, and turn off.

☐ Raise jacks and stow any leveling boards used.

☐ Secure and/or stow all loose articles inside coach, such as hanging plants, lampshades, knickknacks.

☐ Put vents down.

☐ Secure large TV.

☐ Shut and lock all windows.

☐ Lower rear blind.

☐ Close privacy curtain, lock passenger and driver doors.

☐ Set the alarm, close and lock entry door and dead bolt.

17

WHAT ARE SAFE WAYS TO OPERATE AND USE OUR RIG?

*"Then I saw, and considered it well:
I looked upon it, and received instruction."*
Proverbs 24:32

Hitching and Unhitching

We have talked with many people, and opinions are varied—with some diametrically opposed to one another—when it comes to towing. Some people say they would rather tow a larger trailer with a well-equipped and powerful tow vehicle, while others opt for a smaller towed vehicle behind their motorhome. We have driven both types of rigs, and can find no special reason for choosing one method over the other. We can only say that which-ever method you choose, if proper preparations are made, you can have confidence that your choice has been safely used by many others.

The experience of either enjoying or deploring the full-time life can be centered around your preparation for the requirement of hitching and unhitching. When your hitch is the right one, it is properly mounted, and you have received the proper training for its use, there should be nothing to be afraid of.

We have, however, observed people who either didn't know any better, or who had gone to an unscrupulous dealer—or one who just didn't know the product. Their entire rig (as well as their lives) was in jeopardy. They were pulling their trailer with the wrong class of hitch for the load they were towing, they hadn't properly balanced their trailer, or the dealer had misaligned their hitch to the trailer.

We have also seen trailers that were improperly loaded, greatly affecting the tow vehicle's stability. If the trailer is loaded too heavily in front, the weight on the rear of the tow vehicle lifts the front end off the ground and steering becomes unstable. Also, the headlights become ineffective for the driver and can be blinding to oncoming traffic.

When the tongue weight is too light and the rear of the trailer too heavy, the trailer can sway and cause lack of control. This often occurs at high speeds, in the wind, or when passing large trucks.

Watch for excessive tongue weight on your trailer.

On the rare occasion that you see an RV (generally a trailer) in the ditch—were you to investigate the circumstances—you would probably find that there were generally one or more of the following factors involved:

1. The load was too great—or possibly too unbalanced—for the tow vehicle to properly maintain control in all circumstances.

2. The wrong hitch, or an improperly installed or adjusted hitch, was in use.

3. The trailer brakes were not connected, were not properly adjusted, or were malfunctioning and had not been tested.

4. An unskilled, overconfident, or possibly inattentive driver was involved.

5. There was a tire problem, such as over- or under-inflation, leading to a blowout or severe sway problem.

6. The problem may have been a freak wind, which came up and blew the trailer off the road.

It is for these reasons we believe it is in everyone's best interest and safety that RV travelers—especially full-timers—learn all they can about their RV and its handling. After it is prepared for the road, they should practice handling it in safe areas, such as large parking lots, after hours or on weekends, or on rural roads or open fields.

You can set up pylons or other markers and practice backing, turning, placing your rig in tight spots (so you know its size almost by instinct). Test the brakes by feeling, so that you'll know when they are operating.

After perfecting the proper skills and ensuring good preparation of the rig, the only major, unexpected problem you will have to contend with is the rare freak wind possibility.

Making Your Hitch Selection

For the purposes of this book, we do not intend to give detailed and extensive advice for selecting one hitch (i.e., proper class and weight rating) over another. There are several longtime, well-respected hitch manufacturers, whose products are available. Most of their hitches work in the same manner and can be discussed interchangeably.

The one exception, of which we are aware, is the type of hitch that makes towing the travel trailer similar to pulling a fifth-wheel: the PullRite Hitch, manufactured by Pulliam Enterprises, Inc. You may want to learn more about this before making a hitch choice.

Hitch choice is something you must determine after you make your RV choice. Decide if you will be selecting a hitch for your tow vehicle or trailer, or a hitch for your motorhome to allow you to tow a small car or other vehicle.

There are several approaches to making this choice. First you must know what you want, based either on what you already have (in the way of tow vehicle or camp trailer) or what you intend to obtain. Once you have made the first choice, all other choices are based on that requirement.

For example, if you intend to use your existing four-wheel-drive, full-size pickup to pull a fifth-wheel trailer, you must be prepared to have the trailer undercarriage raised to align its frame with the higher tow vehicle. Or, if you plan to use your existing, light, utility pickup to tow a fifth-wheel, you must be prepared to downsize your requirements to the maximum size this truck can handle—generally a "lite-weight" trailer. Locate a dealer whom you can trust, and ask him as many questions as you can, to satisfy any area you don't understand.

A properly aligned and adjusted equalizing hitch—designed to distribute the trailer's tongue weight equally to both the front and rear axles of the tow vehicle—will keep both your tow vehicle and trailer frames level to the ground. Watch for the following signs that indicate a properly installed hitch:

- It will not cause your rig to lean right or left.

- It will not cause the trailer to dip in the front or the rear, nor the tow vehicle to be lower in the rear or higher in the front.

- It will not try to control the steering of the tow vehicle while it is in motion.

A fifth-wheel hitch should meet all of the above requirements as well. Additionally, the hitch-pin weight of the fifth-wheel trailer should not exceed the weight rating of the tow vehicle. Be sure of the following:

- On level ground, the trailer frame and the truck frame should be level, with equal clearance along the truck bed rails from front to rear.

- The center of the pin on the fifth-wheel hitch should be at, or near (within six inches) the center of the axle on the rear drive wheels.

- When the tow vehicle is in a sharp turn—90 degrees or greater, in either direction—the front corners of the fifth-wheel trailer should easily clear the back of the cab as it turns.

- The hitch-pin of the fifth-wheel trailer should always have positive weight on it, and the trailer should be loaded and balanced according to the specifications of the manufacturer (i.e., the back of the trailer should never weigh more than the front. This weight error will cause the trailer to pull up on the hitch-pin).

Tires and Proper Inflation

You should be aware that, as a full-timer, your entire home and its safety rests upon a foundation—your tires. Thus you will not expect these rubber and steel (or nylon) marvels of engineering to last forever or be impervious to the environment. You will take measures to ensure their longevity.

There are several things you can do to ensure a long life for your tires, and help to prevent them from letting you down unexpectedly:

- Carefully note the weight that is on each wheel. Go to a commercial scale and obtain this information after loading your RV as you plan to live in it. Your tire dealer can supply you with a chart listing proper inflation values for the weight on each tire. Keep these values handy whenever you are checking your tires.

- Keep a watchful eye on the proper inflation as recommended by the chart.

- Watch the rate and type of wear at each wheel. At the first sign of uneven wear, you can save money—and possibly a blowout or flat tire—by having the dealer check the problem.

- Be sure to keep a record of the last time your tires were rotated, and where each tire has been in the rotation. Whenever the tires are rotated, re-inflate each on to the proper value according to the chart you obtained above.

- Obtain wheel/tire covers for the tires that will be exposed to direct sunlight while you are parked. Long-term exposure to ultraviolet light is damaging to the rubber of the tires. Some travel trailer tires (marked ST for Special Trailer) have a built-in ultraviolet protection in their formulation, so you might want to look for them in your trailer's size range. We wonder why the tire industry doesn't make the same formulation for motorhome tires.

It is impossible to prevent tire failure due to road hazards and manufacturing defects. However, it is up to you to use your tires within the boundaries of the manufacturer's specifications. It is also easier to avoid damaging your tires due to road hazards by driving at speeds commensurate with the road conditions. You will have more time to react to the hazards on the road if you keep your speed down. You will be much more able to avoid potholes, broken pavement, rocks, and other debris on the road if you give yourself more time to see and react to these "tire killers" before you drive into them.

Freeway Driving

If you have never lived in an urban area, where driving in freeway traffic is a necessity, the operation of your RV in this kind of congestion can be very traumatic. The Southern California freeway system is intimidating to even the most jaded of drivers, not to mention those from a more rural area of the country. If you plan any excursion into those areas of the country where you will be required to drive on unfamiliar freeways or expressways, try to make your plans coincide with a lull in the traffic. Never attempt to drive in the early morning, weekday traffic when the work-a-day drivers are on their way to work. Try to avoid traveling the freeways at the noon or lunch breaks, or from 3:00 to 6:30 p.m. Deanne says that if, additionally you don't drive at night, it looks like you'll have to enter and leave Los Angeles between 10:00 and 11:00 a.m., or between 2:00 and 3:00 p.m. Not much choice; she advises it would be easier to take along a friend who is used to the traffic in this bumper-car environment.

As a full-timer, you will have the luxury of traveling anytime you want to. Why should you choose those times when so many others have to use the freeways? Admittedly, you have every right to the road that they have, but why not use the roads in the midmorning. Or, plan to arrive at your campground the night before, so you can take your time getting to the attraction that has brought you into that area.

Traffic Problems

When driving through large cities, get up-to-date maps of the area, the cities, and its freeway system. Then study and plan your route beforehand. A passenger should act as a co-pilot and navigator with the map open. As you travel, you will find it is easier to recognize your planned route numbers and landmarks if two of you are looking for them. This will also allow time for the driver to be in the proper lane at the right time for exits and other maneuvers.

Always be prepared for any eventuality in this type of traffic. The freeways may be open, with the traffic sailing along, and you'll round a bend and traffic will be completely stopped. Drive with the proper distance between you and the vehicle in front of you (this distance should be equal to the anticipated stopping distance of your rig at the speed you are traveling). Also, plan in your mind, what your contingency moves might be in case of emergency. Which lanes in front of you are clear? How long will it take you to stop? What is beside you? These questions will help keep you alert in this type of traffic, and your mind attentive to any upcoming situation.

We have some very dear friends who refuse to join us in Southern California to see Disneyland and some other local attractions. They are intimidated by the mere thought of the traffic in the area. However, we believe with proper planning and timing, anyone can drive in this type of traffic. Be that as it may, however, they still won't come, so we've offered to drive our truck into the desert and drive their motorhome in for them. They're worth it.

Toll Roads

One of our pet peeves in traveling the freeways and major traffic arteries of this nation are the toll roads. It is not that we resent toll roads as such, or even the fact that they are generally strategically placed where they can intercept the most traffic. Isn't this the area traffic supervisors' prerogative? Tell us, why don't they post the toll rates where you can see them long before you get to the toll booth? It is so frustrating to have to turn around to exit for an alternate route when you find that you are unwilling or unprepared to pay an exorbitant toll for your rig.

Most of these tolls are operated to extract the maximum amount of money from the commercial trucks with their multiple axles and heavy loads. Most toll booth operators will simply charge you, the RV user, the going commercial rate with no recourse except to turn around and leave or pay to use their road or bridge. Most of the toll roads we have taken have been under construction, with driving conditions worse than the free roads.

One year, while driving through south Chicago area on Interstate 80, we were caught in late afternoon traffic and wound up on the I-294 toll section. The road was under complete reconstruction, with all of the pavement broken up, full of ruts, potholes, and loose gravel. When we finally got off this mess—to continue our journey east and north into Michigan—the toll for this approximate five miles of bad road was over $7.50! We were completely flabbergasted to have to pay that amount to use a road that was worse than the trail back to Gene's uncle's abandoned farm house. We have since found that the area you would miss by taking the toll road is generally much more interesting and usually worth the slower pace.

What Speed and How Far

Speaking of a slower pace, for the most part, we have found that the best distance to travel in one day is not more than 300 to 350 miles. This distance in normal weather amounts to six to eight hours' driving time, at an average speed of approximately fifty miles per hour.

If something interests us or if one or both of us have tired more quickly than we expected, we will quit driving earlier. We prepare supper, and just relax for the evening. Although we do still work, writing and traveling on tour for the concerts that Deanne presents in churches throughout the U.S., we keep our schedule such that we can travel in this leisurely manner. Not only for safety, but for our health as well.

A note from Deanne: I don't drive the motorhome. Not because I don't know how, but because I am very concerned that everything we own is right along with us. If I were to have a mishap of any kind that required us to leave the motorhome for a time while repairs were made, where would we go? At what cost? Thus, the rule we follow is that if I am not to drive, I will also not make the choice about when we will stop. When Gene is tired, we rest. If I don't like that, I can get behind the wheel and go on. So far, we have had no problem with this decision. He appears tired about the same time as I.

Inclement Weather Driving

In the Preface to this book, we mentioned driving in the rain as one of our pleasurable pastimes. If traffic conditions are right, your rig is in good repair, and your speed is maintained commensurate to the road and weather conditions, you may find that this is also a good time for you to travel.

We have traveled in the rain, wind, and snow, and sometimes in the rain, wind, and snow simultaneously. But we do not *plan* to travel in these conditions. Often, we have been on our way somewhere and the weather simply caught up with us, or we drove into the inclement weather area unintentionally. As we stated above, if your rig is in good repair, the tires are sound, and you have adequate supplies, you can continue driving in bad weather if you want to. The worst thing that can happen, short of running off the road (and you shouldn't be driving that fast) is that you will have to stop at a station, a road side rest area, or a truck stop, and wait out the weather. We come to look at these situations as new adventures.

Animals and Other Driving Hazards

Animals on the highways are also something to consider as you travel. In many rural areas of the country, you must be alert for the deer and other big game (cows and horses, not to mention unwary children, joggers, or hikers) who may wander unto your pathway.

One year, while traveling through the hills of northwestern Arkansas, we had a near mishap that still gives us cold shivers. It was mid-afternoon, and we were traveling north toward Joplin, Missouri with about two hours of driving left. We rounded a bend in the road, and drove down a hill. Deanne laughed at two cute little black puppies playing off to the right at the bottom of the hill. Just as Gene looked over to see them, one of them broke free and ran, with the other one right on his tail—smack onto the highway! Deanne screamed, and they disappeared from Gene's view as he jammed hard on the brakes.

Because we were only traveling about twenty-five to thirty miles per hour, the quick braking allowed us to slow down enough. The puppies emerged safely on the left side of the rig, still rolling and playing, completely unaware of their near disaster. We learned to slow down when kids and animals are playing alongside the road.

Handling Long/Heavy RVs

Negotiating hills is also a skill you must master as an RV operator. Knowing your rig and your own skill as a driver will enable you to plan your routes. You can then avoid those hills and mountainous areas that make you nervous or uncomfortable. Smart people know and accept their personal limitations and work with them. If you do not feel that you can drive safely through the mountains, plan your route to arrive at your destination from another direction.

When you are driving in mountainous areas, or must negotiate long, downhill grades, be sure of your brakes before starting down. Most highways have a brake-check area for truckers to examine their brakes before starting down a long grade. If you have been using your brakes heavily up to that point, it is wise to pull off and check to see if they are too hot to start down. A few minutes' wait, to allow them to cool, should be a safe tradeoff for the alternative.

Warning

> *Never place your foot on the brake pedal and ride it all the way to the bottom of the grade. You may find that you have no brakes at all, about halfway down the grade, due to overheating. Your brakes may even burst into flames, becoming totally useless.*

Also, you will normally find warning signs at the beginning of long, downhill grades, telling you of the percent of fall (4%, 5%, 6%, or more, with the higher numbers indicating the steeper grades). These warnings advise you to place your vehicle in a lower gear to help maintain a slower speed.

The proper use of your brakes in this situation is: While at the beginning of your descent, you should apply the brakes hard to bring your rig to a slow, comfortable, and controllable speed. Then you should place the tow vehicle (or motorhome) into a lower gear. Now, completely release the brake pedal to allow air to circulate the brake bands and pads for cooling. If your speed begins to pick up again, reapply the brakes to bring your speed down, and if necessary go to a still lower gear to maintain your speed.

NOTE

Because diesel engines do not have any engine braking ability while coming down a hill, engine brakes (like the Jake brake) have been designed to aid in braking on steep grades. They utilize the exhaust system to achieve this braking power. There are other engine brakes available; some even for gasoline engines, as listed in Appendix B.

Whenever you are traveling in hilly or mountainous areas, be aware of those cars (and trucks that have more power, and are trying to maintain a schedule) that are behind you and are looking to pass. In some states, there are laws regarding impeding the normal flow of traffic. These laws state that if a slow-moving vehicle has three or more vehicles behind it (the number varies from state to state), at the first opportunity, that vehicle must pull off the road and allow the others to pass. This is the reason for so many "pull-offs" on most mountain roads.

Because we are not attempting to meet any schedule or set any records in going over the mountains, we always pull off for other drivers. We would never forgive ourselves if, because of our disregard for their frustration, someone was to make a foolish mistake in trying to pass at the wrong time or place, and have an accident. We usually receive friendly waves and/or grateful toots on the horn as these drivers pass us.

Stabilizing and Leveling Your Coach

After all of this travel, you are sure to be ready to settle down for a good night's sleep. Before you can do that, if you plan to operate your refrigerator, your coach will have to be at least somewhat level. This will also ensure peaceful sleep. If your stop is merely for an overnight stay, you probably won't bother with unhitching and putting your jack-stands in place. However, leveling of some sort will still be in order.

Automatic Levelers

Don't be jealous if you have chosen to pull a trailer or fifth-wheel, but as we tell this story, you can marvel at the availability of modern technology. Deanne's sister decided to travel with us for an overnight trip to another city. She has always been an advocate of the fifth-wheel for full-timing, but even she was impressed by the convenience we had while preparing our camp.

This was to be a dry (or "coyote") camp, without electrical or water hookups. We simply pulled the motorhome into our chosen spot, set the brakes, lowered the leveling jacks, turned off the engine and declared: "We're camped!"

There are several manufacturers of these automatic and semi-automatic jacks, and they are now available for trailers, fifth-wheels, and almost every size of motorhome. They are quite expensive, however, especially when compared to jack-stands and boards. Also, don't believe it when you hear that boards and chocks will be outdated. Unless you only make camp in level campsites, you will often need to place additional boards under one or more of the jack feet to attain enough height to level the coach. Carry some with you.

Sometimes we've stayed in spots that were incredibly uneven. Even after dropping our jacks, putting boards under them, and going through tricky maneuvers, we still had to sleep with our heads at the foot of the bed to keep the blood from rushing to our heads.

Trailers

With a standard pull trailer, you will want to level it using either built-in jacks or jack-stands at the corners.

Warning

> *Always be sure to use wheel chocks before un-hitching or attempting to raise, jack, or level your trailer.*

If there is too great a tilt from side to side, you may want to pull the trailer onto some stacked boards before putting the jack-stands in place. Once you have unhitched the trailer from the tow vehicle, it will be easy to level and stabilize. This assumes you have installed a set of level indicators at some point—generally at one front corner—on the trailer.

The bubbles on the indicator will tell you how much you need to raise or lower each corner of the trailer. Adjust the jack-stands for each corner of the trailer frame; then lower the tongue jack until you can place the rear jack-stands under the frame. With them in place, again raise the trailer with the tongue jack until the front stands can be placed. Once they are set in place, lower the tongue jack, and the trailer will be level and stable.

Fifth-wheels

A fifth-wheel is leveled much like the standard trailer. Many of these units have slide-outs, and must be very stable, without twists in the frame, before operating the slide-out mechanism.

When you place your fifth-wheel in an uneven space, you often make unhitching difficult. Then you must use boards under the tow vehicle's rear wheels to level or realign the hitch to the hitch-pin on the trailer. Remember, it will require the same amount of leveling (or more) to re-hitch the trailer.

Today, there are several new items available to alleviate most of the frustration and work required in this situation. Pulliam Enterprises, manufacturers of the PullRite towing system, have developed an innovative fifth-wheel hitch. It allows the hitch head to tilt side-to-side to accommodate this problem. Automatic levelers and manually-controlled power jacks are also available for the fifth-wheel.

Section IV.

Enjoy Yourself!

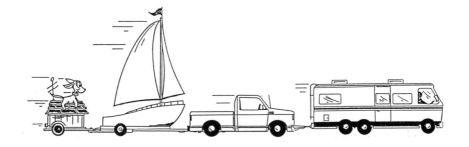

18

LIFE ON THE GO, WITHOUT A TIMETABLE!

"And whatsoever ye do, do it heartily, as to the Lord, and not unto men ..."
Colossians 3:23

Off-Season Camping

For many full-timers, taking advantage of the reduced numbers of people (not to mention the discounted camping fees) in a campground during the off-season, is a way of life. As we mentioned before, the only reason many campgrounds can remain open for the entire year is because of their use by full-timers during the "slack" season.

This is a period when full-timers can make complete use of the park facilities without the noise and hubbub of the summer crowds. It is also a time when one can relax and plan for the following travel year—and reflect on the last.

A caravan piggy-back ride.

Camping in Non-Campgrounds

Many of us are on tight budgets and find that there is sometimes a lot of month left at the end of the money. When travel funds run short, we have the option of staying in less expensive places until the money catches up.

Camping in non-campgrounds is generally no problem if your RV is self-contained; and the following possibilities are tried and tested by many of us:

Often we have spent nights, while traveling, in large truck and rest stops. We have heard warnings against staying in such unsecured areas. While we would feel a little uneasy were we to park where the cars parked—we have learned to feel very comfortable snuggled between the large trucks. We feel safe knowing that there are generally a few truckers awake and alert—some moving in, some moving out—while we and others sleep. All we had to do was learn to sleep through the noise of arriving and departing rigs. But that noise is just what provides us our sense of security—kind of like hearing the rain on the roof. We sleep peacefully.

Other than these overnight stays, we have spent longer amounts of time boondocking in the desert. Sometimes we park in front of friends' homes or on their property, and they have graciously provided electrical hookup to their stationary system. These visits are precious to us, because they allow us a lengthy stay without putting our friends out of their own space.

We generally offer to help with any work that is to be done, in exchange for our hookup there. Although such friends usually decline this proposition, we find ourselves joining them, in doing things that make life easier for them anyway. A great way to visit—and an assurance that we will be invited back!

Gene has done this so often that we get letters from people saying, "We're keeping a list of things we want Gene to do when you get here." Deanne likes to do dishes (she knows it's crazy, but finds it a time to contemplate, since no one ever wants to come and join her). Her sister always says that we should hurry and get to their house because she's keeping the dirty dishes in the hall closet, and it's getting full.

Cold-Weather Camping

Many full-timers (as well as other hardy RV aficionados) like to spend time in cold weather country enjoying winter sports—skiing, sledding, tobogganing, snowmobiling, ice fishing, or hunting. With proper preparation of the RV and use of the right clothing, this kind of camping can be safe and enjoyable.

For safety's sake, plan for, and take enough food and a spare propane tank for heating in case you are snowed-in past your planned return time. It is also wise to let someone know where you are going and when you plan to return from these trips. A sudden storm or an injury can be life-threatening, especially if no one is aware of your whereabouts, or is expecting your return.

Camping Manners

If you observe and listen while in a campground, you will quickly be able to spot those RV travelers who are aware and considerate of others. They are the ones whose arrival or departure time is planned to coincide with the normal waking hours of their neighbors. If they do have to depart early or arrive late, they at least do their hooking and unhooking chores during waking hours. Those who arrive late and try to park, level, and hook up (at the top of their voices) sometime near midnight, may find themselves with no one rushing to meet them during their stay.

Considerate RV dwellers are also the ones who take their loud music and noisy conversation indoors around bedtime, so as not to disturb others. They keep Fido or Tabby on a leash and lead them away from your doorstep before they do their duty (not afterward), and carry a pooper scooper with them—and use it.

Flexibility

Make No Concrete Plans

Whiners and complainers generally don't seem to make good full-timers. As a full-timer you will find that the best laid plans will indeed go awry. Often we have planned to stay in a particular campground, or in a special spot in a campground, only to find it unavailable. However, we have also found that sometimes when our plans were thwarted, the alternative turned out to be better than what we had planned.

The whole of the full-timer experience can be likened to an unwritten adventure book, with chances for new and different experiences occurring each day. So, as we have stated, plan, but be flexible concerning the chapters in *your* book.

Bad Campgrounds

One reason we keep a daily logbook of our activities is that it provides a way for us to evaluate the different campgrounds and places we stay. This is not for the benefit of any organization, but for our own remembrances.

Whenever we return to an area, we can quickly glance at our previous opinion of the campground and determine whether or not we want to stay. Sometimes, if a particular campground has been bad, we will still give them another chance, to see if they have improved. Also, we have decided that we can put up with some extremely bad campgrounds if the price is right and it is only for one night. We just go inside and shut the door.

Guns—Yes/No/Maybe

Entire books have been written, and arguments raged concerning this subject, so we will not do an exhaustive investigation here.

We have decided that the chances of doing harm to someone we love outweigh the times we have needed to use a gun for our protection. The risks are too great to warrant keeping a gun. This determination is not based upon any prejudice against guns; we agree with what our basic rights afford us by the Constitution. We also don't mean to say that anyone who decides to carry a gun with them is not right in their decision.

Guns don't kill; people kill. And people don't always use guns to do it. Also, there is the argument that states when it becomes illegal for the individual citizen to own a gun, only the criminals will have them. It is clearly a very emotional and controversial subject.

We met a man in a campground in Arizona who once pointed what was actually an unloaded shotgun at someone who came to his RV door one night. He considered the gun well worth what it did for him. The intruders backed off, not wanting to know whether the shotgun was loaded or not. But we have wondered what would have happened if they had called his bluff. He could have been seriously injured, but maybe he would have been anyway.

In sum, we will all do what our fears, prejudices, and experiences have taught us to do.

Continuing Your Education

The very fact that you are reading this book is a point in your favor concerning education; and Gene believes that continuing such education (especially about your lifestyle) is an ongoing reality. Legislation, the latest innovations in the RV industry, new ways to travel, and fresh places to visit, afford us a constant stream of information. We are wise to keep up with it, as it makes our lives fuller and our travels more exciting.

Knowledge About the Latest Improvements for Your Lifestyle

Because the home you live in is an example of the latest in technology, your education—or at the very least, your familiarity with that technology—will help maintain your freedom. Who of us can walk through a campground and completely ignore the latest style, or newest RV—or even the neighbor who is working diligently on his rig? This is the full-time life at its finest: learning something new, or passing on to someone else information about the experiences you have acquired.

Periodicals

Gene devours every book and/or magazine pertaining to RVs, or topics even germane to this life. He even reads catalogs, looking for interesting ideas to adapt to this lifestyle. Many of the ideas, adaptations, and changes that we have incorporated into our RV to make it into a full-time home have come from this ongoing research.

Camping/RV Interest Groups

The reading of these periodicals will introduce you to the myriad of different groups who are organized to promote special interests and types of camping or recreational vehicles. Get to know these people. They have our best interests at heart.

Travel Associations

Many membership campgrounds also provide reduced-rate group travel packages and accommodations for their members. These associations also provide monthly newsletters and/or magazines with informative articles about various places of interest. Gene finds that they often contain RV-related facts and articles. One never knows where the next bit of information will come from.

Everyone Wants To Go

Time has passed, and we have traveled many miles, met many new friends, and seen places we would never have seen, had we not been brave enough to try. Sometimes we look at one another and wonder how long we will live over wheels that continually turn.

It is then we smile and say that even if, for some reason, it has to end tomorrow, we have done things that many will never do—and have built memories that cannot be replaced. We are glad we came.

Our thoughts hearken fondly back to the days when all of our household goods were spread on our lawn and we held garage sales. It was then that we found ourselves getting to know neighbors we hadn't met in the seventeen years we had lived in our home. Buyers of our things would say, "Where are you moving to?" When we pointed to the motorhome, parked on the pad beside our house, we often heard, "Can I ride along in your wheel well? I'll be good, and won't make any trouble!"

Baby Grey

Then the day came—in 1988—when we were staying in Colorado, on our way to Missouri to visit some longtime friends from grade school. One night as we went to bed we heard a kitten crying. We remarked on where it might be, and finally decided it must belong in the neighborhood somewhere.

The next night (in Kansas) and the night following (in Joplin, Missouri) we again heard a kitten. We don't know why we never guessed it was the same kitten.

Finally, as we prepared to move on to Michigan several days later, Gene had to examine the undercarriage of the motorhome and we heard the kitten again. Gene peered up into a little platform that is formed where the tag axle is attached to the body, and saw two tiny eyes shining back at him. Here was a little lady who was dedicated to giving up everything to see the world. She had abandoned society's way of life and climbed into the wheel well.

Gene tried to coax her out from the little home she had made, and finally resorted to a broomstick. By prodding gently, he caused her to spring out and take off across the yard. "A Manx cat—I've always wanted a Manx cat!" our friend, Hope, exclaimed; and off we all went in full chase.

The poor, hungry little thing got herself cornered in the backyard. Hope resorted to heavy gloves and a box to let the kitten know she only wanted to catch her in order to make her part of her life.

It took several days, but as Hope and Mike told us later, love and a commitment to Baby Grey finally convinced her she was safe. She stayed and grew in that nurturing atmosphere.

Then one day, Baby Grey was gone again. Hope told us of missing her kitty, and of the love (and popcorn) they had shared in front of the fire on cold evenings. And she hoped Baby Grey was all right.

But she knew she was a traveler. And loving is letting someone go—to live their lives as they want—to make mistakes and seek successes as their heart leads them.

We wonder if Baby Grey crawled up into someone else's wheel well, and is again heading down a road. If so, we can understand her wanderlust. For we know that once you travel, it gets into your blood. Maybe we will see her out there somewhere again.

Then we will wrap our arms around her and weave our lives into hers once more until we part again. For as the cartoon Ziggy says, "The good thing about saying goodbye is that it gives you a chance to say hello again."

So, to Baby Grey and the rest of you—we'll see you on the road; look for us! We're the ones who are driving a motorhome (Gene's favorite pastime), and listening to a football game (his favorite sport). Deanne will have the Sunday paper (her favorite relaxation reading) spread across her side of the driving area, and popcorn (her favorite food) will be in the microwave. It will probably be raining (our favorite weather), and she will probably be humming a song:

For it is in this we believe: "We've only just begun . . . to live!"

APPENDICES

Appendix A

Helpful Addresses and References
RV Clubs and Organizations

Association of RV
Residents, Inc.
P.O. Box 1454
Clermont, FL 32711

Ass'n of Part and Full-
Timers—Home on Wheels
(APFT-HOW); $20/year

Alpenlite Travel Club
P.O. Box 9152
Yakima, WA 98909

(509) 452-3524

American Clipper Owners' Club
514 Washington St
Marina Del Ray, CA 90292

(213) 823-8945
(213) 823-6433

Avion Travelcade Club
P.O. Box 236
De Bary, FL 32713

(407) 668-6219

Barth Ranger Club
P.O. Box 768
Milford, IN 46542

(219) 658-9401

Beaver Ambassador Club
20545 Murray Rd
Bend, OR 97701

(503) 389-1144

Camper Clubs of America, Inc.
2338 S. McClintock Dr.
Tempe, AZ 85282

Campers for Christ $10/year ($15/1st year)
c/o Jackie Dial
6011 Mountain Rd
Dover, PA 17315

Campers on Mission   (no dues)
Home Mission Board SBC
1350 Spring ST NW
Atlanta, GA 30367-5601

Campground Host Program
Coordinator, Alice Siebecker
Lake Ranger Station
Yellowstone Nat'l Park, WY 82190

Carriage Travel Club, Inc.   (219) 642-3622
P.O. Box 246
Millersburg, IN 46543

Coast-to-Coast   (800) 368-5721
64 Inverness Dr, East   (membership campgrounds)
Englewood, CO 80112

Cortez National Motorhome Club   (818) 444-6030
11022 E. Daines Dr.
Temple City, CA 91780

El Dorado Caravan   (913) 392-2171
P.O. Box 266
Minneapolis, KS 67467

Escapees (SKP's) Club   (409) 327-8873
Route 5, Box 310
Livingston, TX 77351

Family Campers & RV'ers   (800) 245-9755
(Formerly National Campers and Hikers Assn)
4804 Transit Rd., Bldg. 2
Depew, NY 14043-4906

    In Canada: 51 W. 22nd Street
              Hamilton, Ontario
              Canada L9C 4N5

Family Motor Coach Ass'n. (FMCA)   (513) 474-3622
P.O. Box 44209   (800) 543-3622
Cincinnati, OH 45244

Fan Trailer Club   (412) 667-8264
Route 7, Box 348
New Castle, PA 16102

First Xplorer   (810) 346-2771
3950 Burnsline Rd
Brown City, MI 48416

Foretravel Motorcade Club   (409) 564-8367
1221 NW Stallings Dr
Nacogdoches, TX 75961

Good Sam Club   (800) 234-3450
3601 Calle Tecate
P.O. Box 6060
Camarillo, CA 93011-6060

Good Sam Tours   (800) 933-9779
P.O. Box 6060
Camarillo, CA 93011-6060

Good Sam Volunteer Host Program
P.O. Box 6060
Camarillo, CA 93011-6060

Handicapped Travel Club, Inc.   (815) 363-0701
211A Creekside Tr   Bob Skummer, President
McHenry, IL 60050   ($5/1st yr; $3/yr afterward)

Holiday Rambler RV Club
400 Indiana Ave   (219) 862-7330
Wakarusa, IN 46573

International CC Country Club   (503) 998-3712
P.O. Box 207
Junction City, OR 97448

International Coachmen Caravan Club   (219) 825-8245
P.O. Box 30
Middlebury, IN 46540

International Family Recreation Ass'n   (904) 477-2123
P.O. Box 6279
Pensacola, FL 32503

International Skamper Camper Club   (219) 848-7411
P.O. Box 338
Bristol, IN 46507

Kampgrounds of America, Inc (KOA)
P.O. Box 30558
Billings, MT 59114

Lazy Daze Caravan Club   (714) 627-1219
4303 E. Mission Blvd
Pomona, CA 91766

Loners on Wheels (LoW)   (817) 626-4538
808 Lester St
Poplar Bluff, MO 63901

Lost Highways Classic Trailer & Motorhome Club
P.O. Box 43737
Philadelphia, PA 19106

NACO   (800) 647-6066
P.O. Box 26   In MS: (800) 231-2286
Gautier, MS 39553   In Canada: (800) 448-6226
                                              (membership campgrounds)

National RV Owners Club
P.O. Drawer 17148
Pensacola, FL 32522

P-O-S-S-E Club   (800) USA-2000
Call George Jackson (SKP 4562)   (property sitting)
                                              ($10/year)

Resort Parks, Int'l (RPI)   (800) 635-8498
3711 Long Beach Blvd, Ste 110   (213) 595-8818
Long Beach, CA 90807   (membership campgrounds)

Roving Volunteers in Christ's Service   (904) 293-4170
(RVICS) and Selected Volunteers in
Christ's Service (SVICS)
1499 Edgewood Ranch Road
Orlando, FL 32811

Serro Scotty Club   (412) 836-3407
450 Arona Rd
Irwin, PA 15642

Silver Streak Trailer Club   (213) 433-0539
226 Grand Ave, 207
Long Beach, CA 90803

SOWERS   (201) 828-6602
P.O. Box 1914   (no dues)
North Brunswick, NJ 08902

Special Military Active/Retired   (904) 456-8218
Travel (SMART) Club, Inc.   ($18/year)
600 University Office Blvd, Ste 1-A
Pensacola, FL 32504

Sportscoach Owners International   (818) 249-4175
3550 Foothill Blvd
Glendale, CA 91214

Streamline Royal Rovers   (817) 267-2167
808 Clebud Dr
Euless, TX 76040

Thousand Adventures, Inc.   (800) 452-1598
P.O. Box 301
Blair, NE 68008

Thousand Trails, Inc.   (800) 647-6066
P.O. Box 26   In MS: (800) 231-2286
Gautier, MS 39553-0026   In Canada: (800) 448-6226
                                   (membership campgrounds)

U.S. Submarine Vet RVer's   ($5/year—for all who
c/o Lorie Sullivan   serve or who have served
1922 Elizabeth St.   in the U.S. Submarine Forces)
Pueblo, CO 81003

Wally Byam Caravan Club Int'l   (513) 596-5211
803 E. Pike St
Jackson Center, OH 45334

Winnebago Itasca-Travelers   (515) 582-6874
P.O. Box 268
Forest City, IA 50435

Appendix B

RV Services and Businesses

Alaskan Caravan Adventures
2506 Glenkerry Dr SR
Anchorage, AK 99504

(800) 288-5840
Collect: (907) 338-1439
(RV caravans)

Alexander & Alexander
700 Fisher Blvd
Detroit, MI 48202-3053

(800) 521-2942
In MI: (800) 624-7539
(full-timers' vehicle insurance)

Best RV
1104 N. Marshall
El Cajon, CA 92020

(window coverings)

California Coachworks
11801 Westminster Ave
Garden Grove, CA 92643

(714) 554-9001
Blair McCullough
RV repair facility; interior
remodeling and all coach work.

Camping World
P.O. Box 90017
Bowling Green, KY 42102-9017

(800) 626-5944 (Camping World)
(800) 228-2911 (President's Club)
(RV supplies, located in many
areas throughout the U.S. Join
President's Club for 10% discounts
and tours)

Caravanas Voyagers
1155 Larry Mahan St, Ste H
El Paso, TX 79925

(800) 351-1685
In Canada: (800) 637-8872
(RV "Piggyback" Adventures)

Carrs RV Tours
11781 Hunter Ave
Yuma, AZ 85367

(800) 526-6469
(602) 342-6695

Chevrolet Motorhome Chassis Svce Guide
Chevrolet Motors Division
General Motors Corporation
Central Office
30007 Van Dyke Ave
Warren, MI 48090

(800) 222-1020
(Information or service
pertaining to the Chevrolet
chassis—and to order the
"Orange Book" (free) for
your particular chassis.)

Creative World Rallies and Caravans
4005 Toulouse St.
New Orleans, LA 70119

(800) 732-8337

Decelomatic Corporation
4837 E. Indian School
Phoenix, AZ 85018

(602) 956-8200
(Mountain Tamer engine
brake for gas or diesel
engines)

GENERAC
P.O. Box 8
Waukesha, WI 53187

(414) 544-4811
(mobile generators)

Hi-Lo Trailer Co.
145 Elm St.
Butler, OH 44822

(419) 883-3000
(800) 321-6402

JCP Enterprises
17671 Falkirk Lane
Huntington Beach, CA 92649

(RV safes)

John Deere Chassis Products
3133 E. Kemper Rd.
Cincinnati, OH 45241

(800) 648-8838
(for directory of service
locations)

Kyocera Solar Panels
4411 E. Echo Lane
Glendale, AZ 85302

(800) 736-9036
(For details on solar
panels, installation)

National General Insurance Co.
Good Sam Vehicle Insurance Plan
P.O. Box 66819
St. Louis, MO 63166-9856

800 VIP-AUTO (Vehicle
Insurance Plan (VIP).
Available through Good
Sam, Coast-to-Coast.)

Newmar Corporation
355 N. Delaware
Nappanee, IN 46550-0030

(219) 773-7791
(makes motorhomes with slide-outs)

Onan Corporation
P.O. Box 32925
Minneapolis, MN 55432

(mobile generators)

O-RAC Industries
255 S. A St
Springfield, OR 97477

(800) 262-6722
(O-RAC tow dollies)

Pacbrake Manufacturing
P.O. Box 8022
Blaine, WA 98231-8022

(800) 663-0096
(604) 882-0183
(engine brake system)

Peninsula Glass
6005 NE 121st Ave
Vancouver, WA 98688

(800) 468-4323
(206) 892-2029
(double-pane glass)

Point South RV Tours
11313 Edmonson Ave
Moreno Valley, CA 92555

(800) 421-1394
(909) 247-1222

Pro-Shield Rubber Roof System
1602 Birchwood
Fort Wayne, IN 46803

(219) 424-2900

Pulliam Enterprises, Inc.
13790 E. Jefferson Blvd.
Mishawaka, IN 46545

(800) 443-2307
(219) 259-1520
(makers of Pullrite Trailer Towing Systems)

Recreational Equipment Mfg Corp
(REMCO)
4138 S. 89th St
Omaha, NE 68127

(800) 228-2481
Canada (402) 339-3398
(axle locks for towing front wheel drive automatic cars; and drive-line disconnects and transmission lube pumps)

Recreational Vehicle Industrial Assn.   (703) 620-6003
(RVIA)
P.O. Box 2999
1896 Preston White Dr
Reston, VA 22090-0999

Recreational Vehicle Rental Assn. (RVRA)   (National association
3251 Old Lee Highway   of rental dealers)
Ste 500
Fairfax, VA 22030

RV Privacy Window Fashions   (window coverings)
2805 Wilderness Plaza
Boulder, CO 80301

Solarmetrics, Inc.   (800) 356-4751
140 Bouchard St.   (makers of solar battery
Manchester, NH 03103   chargers)

Space Craft Factory RV Sales   (800) 762-2389
Main Office   (makes motorhomes
Route 1, Box 93   with slide-outs)
Concordia, MO 64020

Tracks to Adventure   (800) 351-6053
2811 Jackson, Ste. E   In TX: (915) 565-9627
El Paso, TX 79930   (RV wagontrain tours)

Trails-A-Way Caravans   (800) 346-7572
120 S. Lafayette Rd.   (RV caravans)
Greenville, MI 48834

Travelers Reservation Club (TRC)   (800) 843-4039
P.O. Box 37   (reservation service)
Live Oak, FL 32060

U-Haul International   (800) 528-0361
ATTN: Hitch Program   (They will answer ques-
2727 N. Central   tions about their Hitch
Phoenix, AZ 85004   Program and direct you to

one of their 1100 U-Haul
Centers in the U.S. and
Canada; nationwide
warranty)

University of Nebraska—Lincoln
Division of Continuing Studies
Lincoln, NE 68583-0900

(Centralized Corres-
pondence Study (CCS).
Correspondence study
programs for high school
students, both public and
private.)

U.S. Dept. of Agriculture
(U.S. Forest Service)
Washington, DC

U.S. Department of the Interior
National Park Service
P.O. Box 37127
Washington, DC 20013-7127

Golden Eagle Pass (Under
62); Golden Age Passport
(Over 62); Golden Access
Passport (blind and dis-
abled persons)

Valley Fuel Injection, Ltd.
Unit A-10
33733 King Rd, RR 2
Abbotsford, BC
Canada V2S 4N2

(604) 853-6096
(engine brakes for
diesel motors)

Wallenius Motorships, Inc.
P.O. Box 1232
Woodcliff Lake, NJ 07675-1232

(201) 307-9740
(for taking an RV
to Europe)

WeatherProof Plus
P.O. Box 32474
Amarillo, TX 79120

(800) 766-2066
(rubberized roofs)

Appendix C

Telephone Services

Chevron USA, Inc.
Chevron Travel Card Services
Attn: Customer Representative
P.O. Box 5010
Concord, CA 94524

(Ask about Travel Club
message service)

Discover Card's Register Program
P.O. Box 29019
Phoenix, AZ 85038-9019

(800) DISCOVER
($21.99/year includes credit
card protection service)

Global Telecommunications Co.
1990 S. Anaheim Blvd.
Anaheim, CA 92805

(714) 978-9000
(cellular telephones and
telephone service)

Symphony, Inc.
Dan Busch
31100 Telegraph Rd, Ste. 150
Birmingham, MI 48025

(800) 442-3725
(provides cellular phones, data
interfaces, and credit card verifica-
tion equipment. Custom cellular
service and problem solving.)

Trava-Link
3419 Via Lido, #208
Newport Beach, CA 92663

(800) 824-8497
Message No. 614
($17/month - $.43/minute
$50 refundable charge
$49 non-refundable set-up fee)

Appendix D

Helpful Publications

National Parks Trade Journal
L.W. Blenis Designs
Dept. W-1, 180 Camp Fire Dr.
California City, CA 93505

(Over 100,000 jobs for
working in the wilderness
listed in their directory)

RV West Outdoor Publications
P.O. Box 89
Hayward, CA 94542-0089

(415) 886-9501

Selecting an RV Home Base
TL Enterprises, Inc
29901 Agoura Rd.
Agoura, CA 91301

(800) 234-3450

TL Enterprises, Inc.
29901 Agoura Rd.
Agoura, CA 91301

(800) 825-6861
Trailer Life Magazine,
Motorhome Magazine, Highways
Magazine (Good Sam Publications)

Western Horseman Magazine
3850 N. Nevada Ave.
P.O. Box 7980
Colorado Springs, CO 80933

(303) 633-5524

Woodall Publishing Co.
100 Corporate North, Ste. 100
Bannockburn, IL 60015-1253

(312) 295-7799

Workamper News
201 Hiram Rd.
HCR 34-Box 125
Heber Springs, AR 72543

(501) 362-2637
(Looking for work? Order this
monthly listing of jobs which
suit our lifestyle.)

Blake, Gary and Robert W. Bly, *Creative Careers: Real Jobs in Glamour Fields*. The Wiley Press, New York, 1985.

Hawes, Gene R. and Douglass L. Brownstone. *The Outdoor Careers Guide*. Facts On File Publications, 1986.

Hubbs, Don. *Home Education Resource Guide*. Blue Bird Publishing, Arizona, 1989.

Index